Mass-Market Classics

The Home

A celebration of everyday design

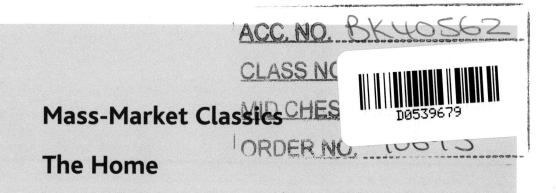

RotoVision

A RotoVision Book
Published and distributed by RotoVision SA
Route Suisse 9
CH-1295 Mies
Switzerland

RotoVision SA,
Sales & Production Office
Sheridan House,
112/116A Western Road
Hove, East Sussex BN3 1DD, UK

Tel: +44 (0)1273 72 72 68
Fax: +44 (0)1273 72 72 69
E-mail: sales@rotovision.com
www.rotovision.com

10 9 8 7 6 5 4 3 2 1

ISBN 2-88046-734-9

Book Editors Gareth Gardner
and Leonie Taylor

Design and artwork Keith Stephenson and
Spike at Absolute Zero°

Photography by Xavier Young

Production and separations in Singapore by
ProVision Pte. Ltd.

Tel: +656 334 7720
Fax: +655 334 7721

Printed and bound in Singapore

Mass-Market Classics

The Home

A celebration of everyday design

Wayne Hemingway

Illustrated by Keith Stephenson

Contents

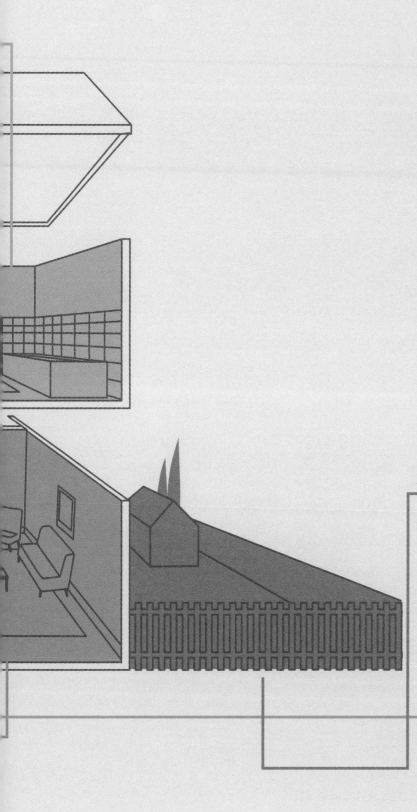

Introduction

Mass-Market Classics is a celebration of the products that the public use, and have used, in their daily lives. Products that have proved their design excellence by sales volume. Products that have created employment, fuelled the growth of home shopping, the development of the high street and retail parks. Products that are, or have been, in our family homes regardless of class or taste. Products that can finally grasp their well-earned 15 minutes of fame, as elitism diminishes and the eminently sensible concept of functionality comes to the fore.

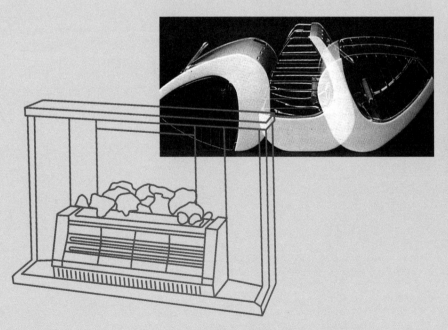

From left, the simple elegance of a convector heater; self-righting electric heater (page 40)

Many of the items in this book haven't been celebrated in print before, for reasons of class and taste. But what is tasteless about products that work and make our lives easier, more comfortable or less expensive? If taste is about showing off your Murano glass vase while hiding your Breville toasted-sandwich maker, then call me tasteless. If class is about not celebrating the universally successful, then I'll come over all communist and expedite the demise of the class system.

There is, of course, value in design as a pure art form. As a result of our obsession with exclusivity, constant change, and our yearning for eye candy, products designed for the intellectual, visual and financially elite will always dominate glossy magazines and coffee table books. The media tend to give disproportionate coverage to Philippe Starck-designed pieces that never touch our lives. It is time to celebrate the everyday, and judge products on their usefulness.

As a designer, it has taken me 20 years to rid myself of elitism and design snobbery. No longer does the fear of the uncool, or vacuous thoughts like, 'What will other designers and the press think?' enter the creative process at my design practice. I have learned to embrace volume and to accept my accolades from members of the public who are willing to invest their scarce resources in my products. Give me a top ten seller at my local interiors superstore rather than a trophy at a swanky design industry awards ceremony any day. This is not some socialist rant but a realisation that ego massaging plays too great a part in the lives of designers. It is time to celebrate ego-free and successful design that the public has bought.

I grew up in a style-conscious, working-class family in 1960s northern England. We embraced change long before the glossies implored us to update last season's fuchsia. It was long before 'consumer porn' magazines advised us that we couldn't live without a Charles and Ray Eames chair or a Bauhaus recliner. This was long before dodgy television make-over programmes took control of our minds, and adverts attempted to brainwash us to 'Chuck out the chintz'.

I observed my family's careful choice of products; selections based on affordability, usefulness and perceived longevity. The purple vinyl sofa and matching shag-pile carpet; the smoked-glass and chrome telephone table and accompanying Trimphone; the built-in, moulded bathroom suite. These were major long-term investments. But thank goodness for the unsung product designers who gave us affordable classics like the three-bar electric fire, the rotary clothes line or drop-leaf kitchen table. Praise be to the designers who gave us access to democratic materials in the form of Tupperware, polystyrene ceiling tiles, textured wallcoverings, beaded door curtains, carpet tiles and paper lampshades. Most of these products have not attained retro novelty status, nor are they being remembered through rose-tinted glasses. They are still sold from the stores and home shopping catalogues that have carried them for decades. G-Plan furniture and Morphy Richards hostess trolleys may have limited value at auction, and are more likely to be found in the rain at a car boot sale than at Sotheby's, but their ubiquitous presence in homes throughout the land is testament to their design success.

The media have an insatiable hunger for new designs, to cram pages and television schedules with products that are intended to fill us with awe and the often financially damaging desire to own them. It is leading to a society where people are slaves to their homes and to change. Surely our homes should be sanctuaries, where we can escape the pressures of modern life, where we are not on public show. This race for newness and false obsolescence has even led to words like 'common' and 'everyday' becoming derogatory terms. *Mass-Market Classics* reclaims the 'common', the 'everyday' and salutes the mundane.

The living room

The living room is aptly named, as it is a space in which we quite literally 'live'. We socially interact, listen to music, watch TV and unwind from life's pressures. The living room is also the spiritual home of flat pack and self-assembly. In the 1960s, classic designs by G-Plan and Schreiber, plus goods from Terence Conran's Habitat empire, became favourites. This room is also the depository for mass-market icons such as beanbags, lava lamps, and sundry nick-nacks.

Self-assembly shelving

The living room has always been a museum for showcasing our possessions; a sanctuary where we can sit among the flotsam and jetsam of our lives. All collections need cabinets and, for the living room, there are self-assembly wall units. Wood-veneer, wipe-clean plastic, steel, chrome and smoked glass multifunctional structures can be assembled in dozens of shape permutations. Anyone can 'design' their own wall storage unit that could take the television, the radio, a rubber plant, commemorative Silver Jubilee plate and ceramic owl.

Some adventurous souls, priding themselves on the stability of their constructions, use their shelving units as room dividers. As well as making designers of us all, this fashion for self-assembly has turned us into do-it-yourself devotees. A Sunday spent struggling with unintelligible instructions and missing screws, splattered with dodgy-looking glue stains, has become part of life. There are, however, manufacturers that deprive us of these dubious pleasures by providing shelving that fits together without screws or glue.

With their flair and love of nudity, the French dispensed with dark wood in the 1960s, encouraging the population to stain their own timber. Meanwhile the Canadians offered us pin-thin supports holding metal shelves with a walnut grain, lithographs, plus enamel end panels on sway-proof chromium-plated steel posts.

Tips for self-assembly

1. Open contents of the box onto the carpet, and lay them out in exact position as shown on the instruction leaflet

2. Impress the wife by ticking off all the contents against the list

3. Play with the dog or child

4. Tear up the instructions as it has been torn by said dog or child

5. Call wife to view the evidence of destroyed instructions and then call in a trusty odd job man

6. Play with your child and dog while the odd job man does his bit

Above, *modular shelving could store all your nick-nacks. This unit was designed by Adrian Heath*

Opposite page clockwise from top, *in Europe the onus was on the consumer to paint or stain the furniture, slender supports were popular with the public; self-assembly used to create an entire wall of storage; metal uprights with wooden shelves and cupboards were a popular combination*

The sofa set

Sofas mean a lot to people. They dominate furniture stores, and we spend a lot of time sitting on them. If we purchase wisely, they are extremely comfortable and last a long time. Many people use them as a design statement or a personal calling card; I use them as a place to fall asleep in front of television. When I think of sofas, I don't think of Cappellini chrome-legged minimalism, but fat, plumped-up sofas, advertised by well-endowed blondes and a cheesy jingle. They should be your first interior investment. If you can't afford a bed, a sofa will do the trick. If you can't afford a microwave, then the local Chinese delivers for free.

While most people chose the fat sofa, Habitat in the 1970s successfully married the two concepts of fat and lean with their bright tubular framed 'fat minimalist' range. The Germans fell in love with that delightful design evergreen 'chrome and shit-brown combo'. Tasty.

The elderly, infirm, or plain bone idle, took to the 'lazy boy' recliner – a sofa or chair that at the push of a button (or if you are poor, the pull of a lever) sends you hurtling into a horizontal position. Top of the range, boy racer versions these days come complete with refrigerator, telephone and built-in TV channel changers.

From top, this three piece suite provides comfort even if it's not a style statement; a 1974 beige concoction from Habitat

Opposite page, clockwise from top left, Germanic chrome and brown; France's take on modular, from the Quelle catalogue 1979; ribbed pleasure from Habitat in the same year

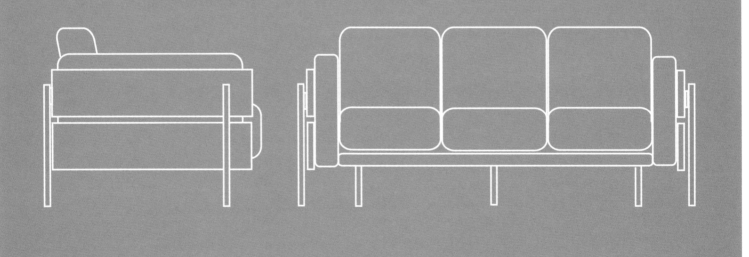

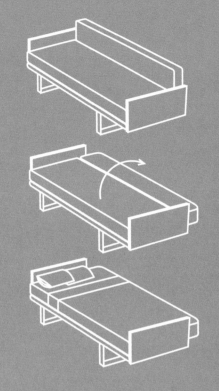

Sofa beds

In an increasingly crowded world, space is at a premium. Probably the most successful space-saving piece of mass-market design is the sofa bed.

The concept of a sofa that, with the pull of a lever or two, transforms into a bed, is a winner in more ways than one. For those who are keen to make their mother-in-law believe that they are too short of bedrooms for a protracted visit, but wish to encourage their pals to stay over, they are a cunning piece of design. When you're watching that racy late night movie with your partner, sofa beds make ideal lovemaking contraptions for those with hard floors and no underfloor heating. They are also a favourite of couch potatoes and bedsit inhabitants.

While the British liked to keep their sofa beds looking like settees, Americans and Canadians came up with a strange sofa/sideboard/bed combo – a 'sobobed' or a 'bedfaboard' or a 'sidebedofa' – and coined the phrase 'dual-purpose living'. The Germans came up with cupboard sofa beds and chair beds. Back across the pond, those larger-than-life Americans conceived the double-decker sofa bed. The simplest-thinking award must surely go to Habitat's 1974 stackable version.

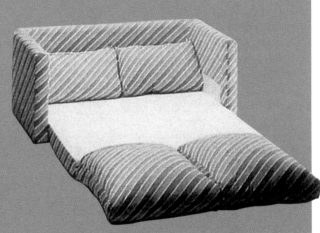

Left and above, the Brits like sofa beds to look like settees, like this one from Marshall Ward in 1986

Clockwise from top left, the joy of dual-purpose living, from Eatons in the mid-1960s; a sofa bed and cupboard combo from Germany; simple foam and strong patterns from German retailer Schwab, 1975; Habitat's simple-to-use and stackable sofa bed, dating from 1974

Beanbags and poufs

Who would have thought that dried beans sewn into a vinyl bag would catch on as a seat? In the 1970s, beanbags were the epitome of style. There were vinyl, leather, plastic, cloth and corduroy versions, and even hybrids like the 'chairbag' and 'tablebag' (a beanbag table in the shape of a chef's hat). For all this supposed innovation, the beanbag wasn't a new concept: bean-filled poufs had been a staple in my nan's house for years. There were suede ones complete with images of camels and men in fezzes, obtained when the cruise ship stopped at Tangiers, and leather ones with donkeys from when it moored at Madeira. In the 1970s, poufs got brave and tried out new roles, including the pouf storage stool.

Dispensing with tradition and the sustainability of beans, many companies now use small pellets of foam or polystyrene. Not only does this make the worst mess if they spill out, but according to the US consumer product safety commission there is a more sinister danger: 'Young children and babies can suffocate from inhaling the small pellets of foam filling, if they unzip the beanbag.' Beanbags are no longer cool and 'death by beanbag' is a duff thing to have on your gravestone. Best stick to the 'inspired by beanbag' air-filled versions by the likes of UK designers Inflate, or zippable, stackable future poufs from gadget gurus Innovation.

From top, exotic leather poufs from French retailer Quelle, 1971; beanbags in all shapes and sizes from Montgomery Ward in the UK, 1978

Opposite page, kiddie-sized beanbags were all the range in Britain in the mid-1970s. These colourful examples were made by Habitat

2

Sideboards

As well as shelving, storage in the living room manifested itself in the form of the eminently sensible sideboard. The sideboard must not be confused with the facial hairstyle for men – the sideburn – but it is equally stylish.

In the 18th century, sideboards were marble-topped and used to cut and serve food in aristocratic dining rooms. But they didn't peak until the 1960s, when they became the proud, inlaid teak home of the Sunday dinner service, cut-glass crystal, photo albums and family heirlooms. Entire stereo systems were incorporated into glass-fronted versions and some metamorphosed into television or drinks cabinets. UK manufacturer Schreiber used modernist minimal styling and affordable veneers. Robin Day's 1950s classic for Hille was, to my mind, the pinnacle of sideboardism.

Above, modern design was brought into millions of UK homes thanks to G-Plan furniture and its many copies. This sideboard was sold through Freemans catalogue in 1970

Opposite page, from top, 1950s sideboard by Robin Day for Hille; a selection of sideboards and stereograms from German retailers in the 1960s and 1970s

240 cm

250 cm

225 cm

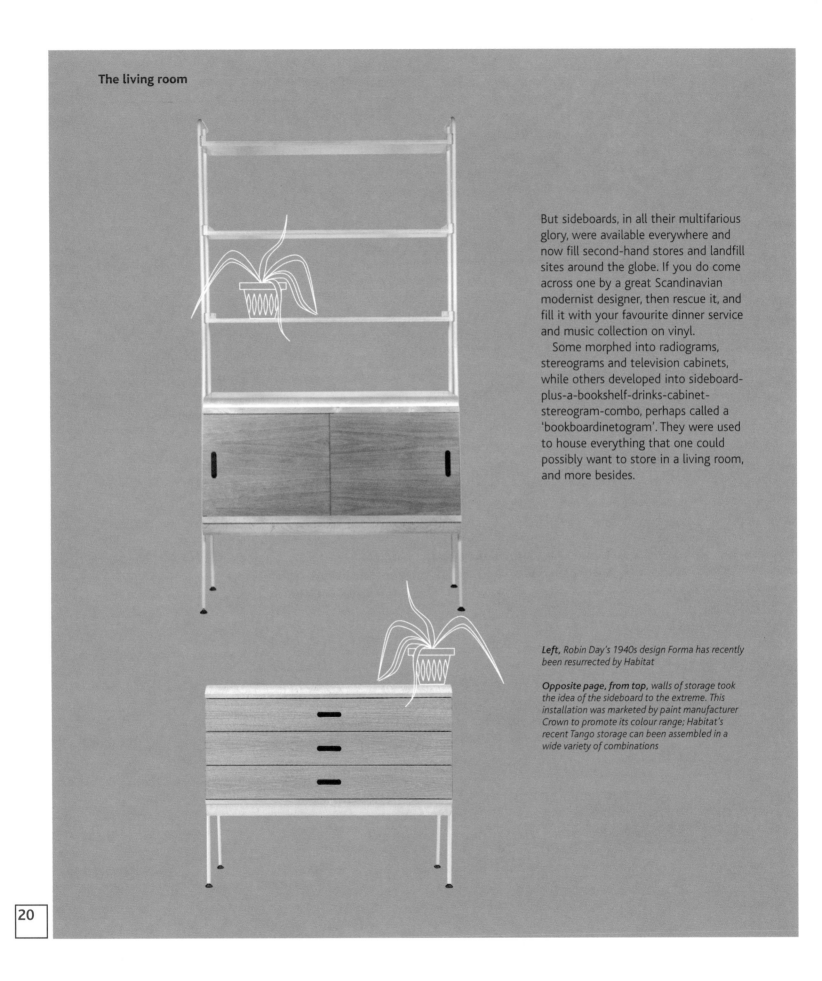

But sideboards, in all their multifarious glory, were available everywhere and now fill second-hand stores and landfill sites around the globe. If you do come across one by a great Scandinavian modernist designer, then rescue it, and fill it with your favourite dinner service and music collection on vinyl.

Some morphed into radiograms, stereograms and television cabinets, while others developed into sideboard-plus-a-bookshelf-drinks-cabinet-stereogram-combo, perhaps called a 'bookboardinetogram'. They were used to house everything that one could possibly want to store in a living room, and more besides.

Left, Robin Day's 1940s design Forma has recently been resurrected by Habitat

Opposite page, from top, walls of storage took the idea of the sideboard to the extreme. This installation was marketed by paint manufacturer Crown to promote its colour range; Habitat's recent Tango storage can been assembled in a wide variety of combinations

Tables for telephones, plants, coffee and special occasions

Before we enter the living room, it is good to hang up one's coat and deposit the umbrella where it will not wet the carpet. The hall set provides all this and more.

When a product goes through a sales explosion and becomes something that almost everyone has, designers always try to come up with a way to add further sales. In the days of the non-mobile phone on a wire (remember them?), some clever person came up with the idea of a telephone table. Telephones were often wired into the lobby, near the front door which, apart from the coat and hat-stand, was traditionally a furniture-free environment. However, the telephone needed to rest on something, as did the telephone directory and – for those long chats with Auntie Joan – a seat was required. And so, the telephone table.

If you were the modern Trimphone or Ericofon-owning type, it was white melamine with a vibrant vinyl seat, or stackable Elena tables or bright plastic Moveables from Habitat. There were also versions for the traditional reproduction-Chippendale-loving masses, enabling the inhabitants of an increasingly communicating world to chat in their lobbies. Telephone tables are still popular in the USA, but they are a bit surreal for my liking. The fitness freaks of Germany preferred telephone shelves. Perhaps they spent less time on the telephone?

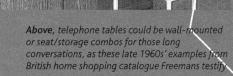

Above, telephone tables could be wall-mounted or seat/storage combos for those long conversations, as these late 1960s' examples from British home shopping catalogue Freemans testify

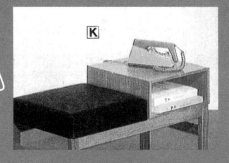

Plant tables took the telephone table's two-tier design to new heights, allowing plants to have their own private space in an increasingly crowded home environment. The keen plant table gardener understands the subtle variations in altitude and how this will effect their potted foliage. Plant table anarchists allow ivy to tumble unbidden from the upper tiers onto the plants below, but this is not something for the purist. For all interior-loving firemen, the plant pole was invented.

Right, 'Plant Life' by Terence Conran for Midwinter, 1956

Below, an array of multi-tiered plant tables from German retailer Neckermann, 1964

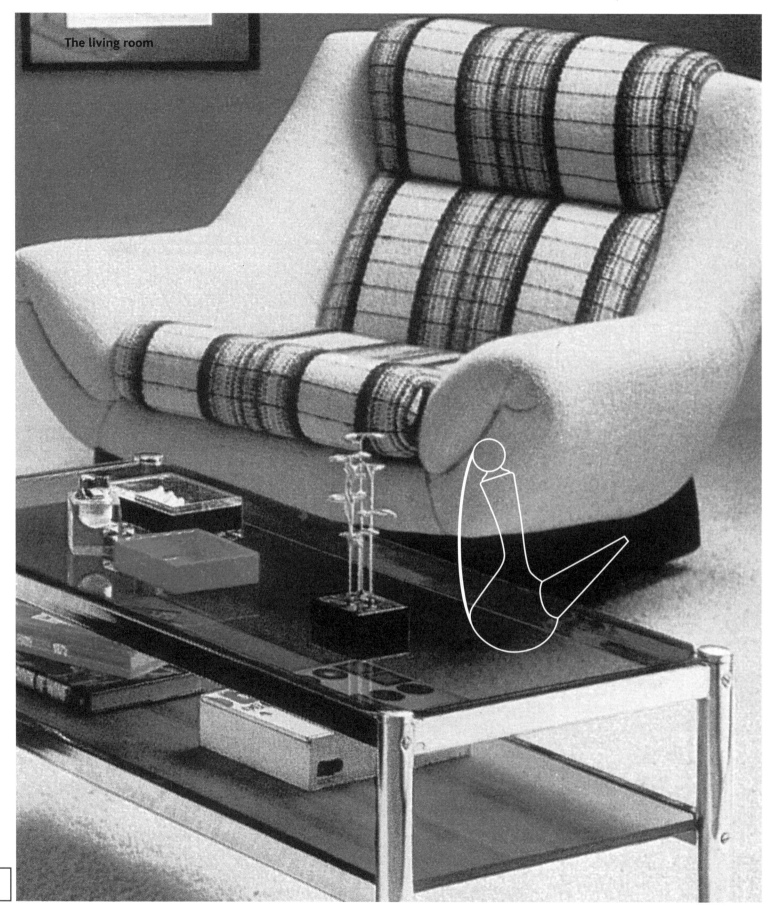

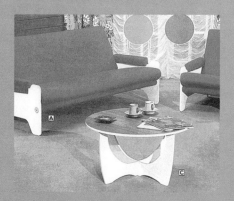

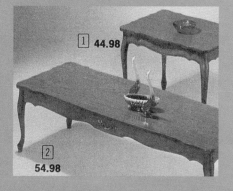

From top, coffee tables provide essential surface space for entertaining guests; occasional tables can stack as nests for storage when not in use; a variety of different heights make occasional tables suitable for a wide range of situations; As well as modern style, traditionally styled coffee tables were popular in the 1970s

Opposite page, coffee tables provide the ideal place to display ornaments and coffee table books

As coffee became the beverage of modern man, relegating tea to flat-cap-wearing pigeon racers in Yorkshire, entrepreneurial retailers spotted a demand for a new accessory – the coffee table. I am not a coffee drinker, and my family has always fancied pigeons, but we embraced the concept of the coffee table in the same way that my non-coffee drinking kids do. They use our various coffee tables as homework surfaces while sitting on the floor watching TV. One of our coffee tables is not suitable for homework as it houses a copy of this fine 'coffee table book' you are reading.

To be up with this low table thing, you need to have all the attributes of a seasoned birdwatcher, the ability to spot subtle nuances. Q: Is it a telephone table? A: No, it doesn't have a seat. Q: Is it a coffee table? A: No, you can tell by its poise and its position away from the sofa. Conclusion: It must be an occasional table. Just like bird twitchers can tell their shanks from their tits, coffee table connoisseurs understand their occasional tables.

While the nest of tables comes in for derision among many design aficionados, one of the first nests was designed by Marcel Breuer (of Bauhaus fame) and manufactured by Viennese manufacturer Thonet from 1926 to 1930. The fun loving Germans turned their coffee tables into the wonderfully named 'disco-table' to house their collections of *Klaus Wunderlich Plays Boney M* records.

A most worrying phenomenon, perhaps with its roots in the 1960s iconic lady-on-all-fours table by Allen Jones, is the popular explosion of glass coffee tables held up by mermaids, dolphins and hippos.

D
La table roulante
320⁰⁰

Smoked glass, chrome and futurism

Barbarella and the raft of 1960s futuristic films and TV programmes led to a mass-market explosion of new materials for our homes. My favourite was brown Plexiglas (a US-developed transparent plastic) which still looks cool, if you can find the rare, unscratched pieces. There's something of a French erotic film-feel about a smoked glass table with chrome legs, topped by a fruit bowl. Or is that me?

The French, with their love of the future, embraced smoked glass and chrome, moulding wonderful coffee and stacking tables, hostess trolleys and magazine racks. The Canadians created majestic self-assembly smoked glass and chrome towers, while the British found it all a bit too continental, preferring to wait till Habitat introduced tech in the 1970s.

Tech was a phenomenon. The love of cheap-to-produce, hollow tubes of metal sprayed jet black, presumably based on some Teutonic principle of minimal elegance, thankfully passed me by. Yet judging by the amount I see in junk stores, it must have sold by the thousand. Tech towers, sofas, wall units and coffee tables, transformed rooms into Playboy-style ladykiller environments, perfectly offset by Athena prints of over-made-up ladies melting phones with their 'red-hot chat'.

Athena prints

Any chrome and tech room isn't complete without an Athena print. Athena in the 1970s and early 1980s brought affordable prints to us all. No house was complete without a red-lipped beauty sucking suggestively on a cherry, or a racy siren morphing into the bonnet of a red sports car. Prints of exotic cocktails on the window ledge of a glamorous hotel room looking out onto Hong Kong Harbour, or images of Parisienne ladies with wide-brimmed hats and high heels, fulfilled dreams of foreign travel.

Mass-Market Classics

D
98⁰⁰

C
Le lot de 3
240⁰⁰

B
La table
99⁰⁰

A
Le lot de 3

F
49⁰⁰

G
Le lot de 3
199⁰⁰

E
198⁰⁰

I
Plateau rond ou ovale
360⁰⁰

J
199⁰⁰

K
265⁰⁰

La même table
existe avec 1 ou 2
plateaux de verre fumé.

Above, *a mélange of steel, chrome and glass
beauties from French retailer La Redoute, 1976*

Opposite page, clockwise from top, *glass and
chrome drinks table from La Redoute, 1976; the
glamour of an Athena print – Long Distance Kiss,
in trademark black, white and red; Habitat's Tech
living room, from 1981*

Wicker, rattan and Lloyd Loom

Picture a blonde beauty in a long dress, sitting in a rattan or bamboo butterfly chair. Add a bit of Vaseline-on-lens-style soft focus, soft-porn photography, and you have an ephemeral style that has somehow lasted.

Some might say that to keep returning to this image is reinforcing female sexual stereotypes. I say that you can stick this politically correct rubbish in your pipe and smoke it – it's good for the world. Rattan is a major source of indigenous income for rural folk in southeast Asia, it is

environmentally friendly, biodegradable and grows in degraded forests and in marginal soil. What's more, it can be introduced artificially to natural forests without upsetting the ecological balance (I knew my geography degree would come in handy).

So bring back those cheap mass-produced copies of Danish designer Nanna Ditzel's iconic 1959 hanging rattan chair.

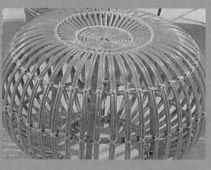

Clockwise from top, wicker given a modern twist by Habitat; butterfly chairs – ideal for conservatories; wicker footstool for ultimate lounge discomfort

Opposite page, suspended rattan inspired by Nanna Ditzel, 1959

The living room

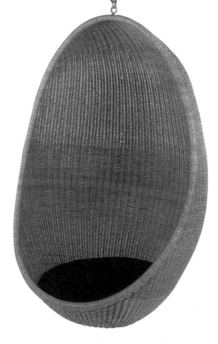

In Britain, Habitat was the first major retailer to introduce a world of wicker to the general public, using rattan and bamboo in their Manau suite and coffee table sets. Habitat mixed it with honey-coloured beech for the iconic Bentwood rocker, and used it in cane lightshades. The retailer also used eastern European willow in some pretty flimsy conservatory sets, but I wish they had stuck to bamboo, described as the 'wood of the poor' in India, the 'friend of the people' in China and simply 'brother' in Vietnam.

The world went rattan and bamboo mad in the 1960s and 1970s, and there must have been few households that

escaped a sofa, shelving unit, dining room set, Ali Baba linen basket (page 72), or footrest in these materials.

However, we can't ignore the noble forerunner of the rattan/bamboo explosion: Lloyd Loom. To me, Lloyd Loom means unsavoury pink-painted commodes thrown out from old people's homes. But to many, Lloyd Loom is the epitome of aristocratic British affordability. Lloyd Loom is simply twisted kraft paper woven into a fabric, reinforced with steel wire and then used on a bentwood frame. It is extremely durable, as some of the original 1917 commodes have proved.

Clockwise from top, why have legs when your chair can hang?; the perfect partner for a rattan chair: a wicker frog; a 1950s Lloyd Loom chair

Opposite page, from top, chunky bamboo used for living room furniture by Habitat, 1977; a perfect interior for a panda

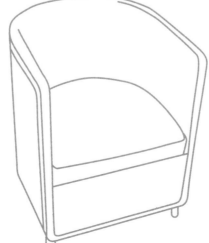

Couch- und Liegendecke
140×200 cm **119.-**
140×240 cm **139.-**
ACRYL Sesselschoner **39⁹⁰**

Sheepskin, 'big foot' slippers and shag pile

It is not just in Wales that sheep and sex enjoy close associations. Many delicate embraces have been undertaken on a skinned sheep in front of a coal-effect fire. Whether it's the caveman in us, a primitive instinct rekindled by watching Raquel Welch in One Million Years BC, or simply because it is comfortable, naked skin feels good next to sheepskin.

Things got a little silly with the foot muff or 'big foot' slipper – a giant sheepskin slipper in which to place both feet while watching telly. Top tip: Don't try standing up quickly to celebrate a goal or home run, or you could end up flat on your face.

Whether it was because sheep became scarce, or maybe they objected to being used as rugs, sheep-alike scatter rugs came to the fore, usually crafted from synthetic fibres. Maybe the idea of scatter rugs was to vary sexual locations around the house. To spice things up further, those randy Germans took to 'zebra-alike', 'antelope-alike', 'buffalo-alike' and 'cow-alike' sheepskins. Phwoar!

Continuing the sexual theme, shag pile came along, looking rather like a sheep subscribing to the Rastafarian religion, but only able to afford a nylon wig. My mum bought a vivid purple one, and covered the floors, walls and doors in it.

Elvis went one better at his Memphis pad by covering his stairs, walls and ceiling in it. In my house, the shag pile always got full of crumbs, spiders and dog hair. When mixed with spilt drinks, it looked like a tramp's hairstyle.

Nowadays we are encouraged not to have shag pile as it harbours the dust mite. Until they prove that this mite is a cause of asthma then join me in starting a campaign to protect the dust mite's natural habitat. SOS: Save our Shag.

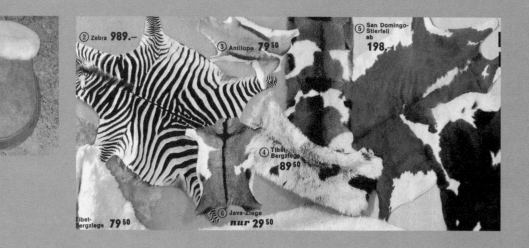

② Zebra **989.-**
③ Antilope **79⁵⁰**
⑤ San Domingo-Stierfell ab **198.-**
④ Tibet-Bergziege **89⁵⁰**
⑥ Java-Ziege nur **29⁵⁰**
Tibet-Bergziege **79⁵⁰**

⑧ **Tibet-Bergziege 198.—**

⑦ **Austral-Schaf ab 49 50**

⑩ **griechischer Hirtenteppich ab 54 50**

Echt Flokati

naturbeige

weiß uni

naturweiß

Above, the luxury of Flokati kept even the most scantily dressed German girl warm in winter. From German retailer Neckermann, 1971

Left, why have one fake fur throw when you could have five? The sexual opportunities were endless...

Opposite page, from top, caveman chic from French retailer Quelle, 1979; fur-effect rugs didn't always have an erotic appeal; a genuine Big Foot slipper; Neckermann took things to extremes with fake zebra, antelope and buffalo hides

Lighting

The volume lighting market was quick to exploit the explosion in lighting design that came out of Italy in the 1960s and 1970s. From the trend for flying saucer-style, to pendants with a UFO aesthetic, to acrylic and chrome 'mushrooms', the way you lit your living room became an important style statement.

Whether the trend was wicker or rattan, Teutonic high-tech, floral country-style, or 1960s futurism, then there was a lamp to match.

Balls of string became pendant lights; bulbs sat on the end of chrome poles; string art was mixed with Perspex to form wonderfully timeless specimens. Strips of plastic or aluminium were fashioned into alien spaceship-like creations. The possibilities were endless.

Clockwise from left, a mushroom table lamp from Habitat, 1974; by 1981 Habitat had embraced the high-tech with this metal standard lamp; an array of paper, glass, wicker and macramé shades from French 3 Suisses catalogue, 1980

Above, standard lamps featuring a range of mushroom-shaped shapes were big with Habitat in 1981. The designs reflected the influence of Italian lighting design from the previous two decades

35

Lava lamps

I don't necessarily like everything in this book, and I don't expect you to like all the things that I have picked. I certainly don't like lava lamps and don't understand their huge appeal, but they are definitely a mass-market classic thanks to the sheer volume of sales and their popular longevity. The lava lamp has come to be one of the iconic images of the 1960s psychedelic movement and the original acid generation.

Designed in the 1960s by British eccentric Edward Craven Walker – a practising nudist, filmmaker and founder of several nudist colonies – lava lamps became massively popular in the 1970s, died off a bit in the high-tech 1980s and then took off again in the nostalgia-mad 1990s. Lava legend has it that the inventor was inspired by a home-made light he saw in a pub in 1963, made out of a glass cocktail shaker and some tin cans. Learning that the maker of this primitive light was dead, Walker made a commercial version and sold the major US distribution rights to Adolph Wertheimer who came up with the name Lava Lite Lamp. A fortune was made, sales then dipped in the 1980s and the European rights were sold to a small business owned by Cressida Granger and based in London's Camden Market. She formed Mathmos and relaunched the lava lamp in the 1990s to great success, generating sales of over £17m in 1999, and launching new products, including colour-changing bricks and gently glowing soft pebbles.

In the US, in excess of 400,000 are now sold annually. You can even get ones featuring Absolut Citron vodka and Microsoft Windows XP. You name a corporation and there will be some unimaginative marketing executive who has suggested a 'Lava lamp to show how kooky our brand is'. I say: 'Get a life'.

A spin off from the lava lamp that became equally ubiquitous is the fibre-optic lamp. It works by magic (or so it seems).

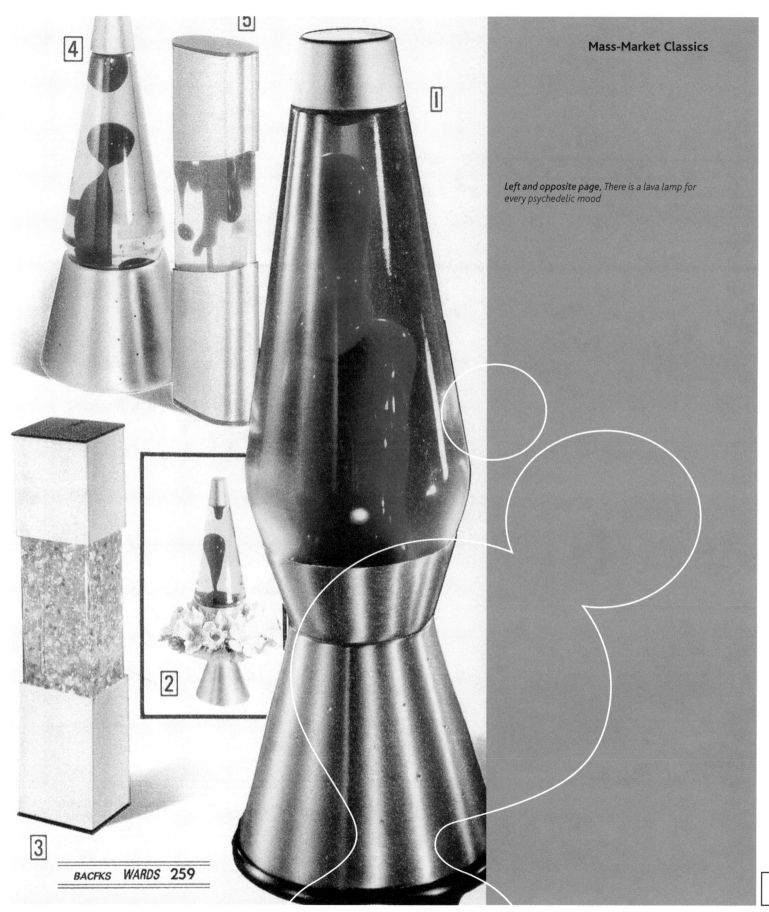

Left and opposite page, There is a lava lamp for every psychedelic mood

BACFKS WARDS 259

Carpet tiles

I never understood why carpet tiles went out of fashion. At first they were replaced by wall-to-wall carpets. I accept that with wall-to-wall you cannot see as many joins, but so what? What's wrong with seeing joins? Joins are beautiful things. What's more, if you spill something indelible or make a nasty stain on your carpet tile, then you can simply whip it up and swap it. Try doing that with your luxury Axminster.

If you need to get under the floorboards to check on the remains of your dead cat, or simply to lay rat poison, then moving your three-piece sofa and rolling up your heavily tufted broadloom is not the easiest task.

When bare floorboards started to accompany Laura Ashley wallpapers, dado rails and festoon blinds, and lofts exploded (not literally) with all their industrial concrete flooring, the market for wall-to-wall carpet was decimated. And carpet tiles became something remembered in television nostalgia programmes.

This mass-market classic has shown its true value by making a dramatic comeback in the 21st century. As technology has allowed modern design to enter the carpet tile world, and as our increasingly wired existence necessitates getting under those floorboards, the carpet tile is enjoying a resurgence.

Clockwise, from top, Milliken's Pattern Express range; 1980s chic from Milliken's Premier Vision range; Milliken's GoModular designed by Wayne and Gerardine Hemingway; colourful and flexible flooring from French retailer Quelle, 1972

Opposite page, Checkertex flooring, as advertised in UK magazine Ideal Home in the 1970s

Coal-effect fires, three-bar electric and convector heaters

Coal-effect fires are about as kitsch as things come, but they are a true hardy perennial that fuel (if you'll excuse the pun) thousands of businesses today, and provide a focal point for living rooms the world over. Some bright spark (sorry about this) had the simple idea of putting orange lights and slow moving fans behind a moulded fibreglass cover would create an uncanny resemblance to a coal fire. There's no need to get your hands filthy, or to fill the air with sooty smoke; just sit back and enjoy the beauty of a real fire.

I understand the reluctance to venture outside on a cold wet evening to bring in filthy coal, but it's beyond me why an unobtrusive radiator can't suffice. You can't argue, however, with sales volume – and these designs, both electric and gas versions, are long-term hot sellers (here I go again). Today manufacturers have got them looking pretty realistic, but they don't fool me.

The Braemar is the all time 'Daddy' with its shelves that can be filled with (and if you are going to partake then you might as well go the whole hog) horse brasses, various non-functioning copper kettles and miners' lamps, and some treasures from the Franklin Mint. It's guaranteed to provide a bit of baronial grandeur to the smallest of homes.

From top, not only a source of heat, coal-effect fires are a useful place to store your trinkets; coal-effect, stone-effect and wood-effect come together in perfect harmony

Right, a modest 1970s example from Dimplex

Opposite page, electric heaters in all shapes and sizes from Valor, 1970

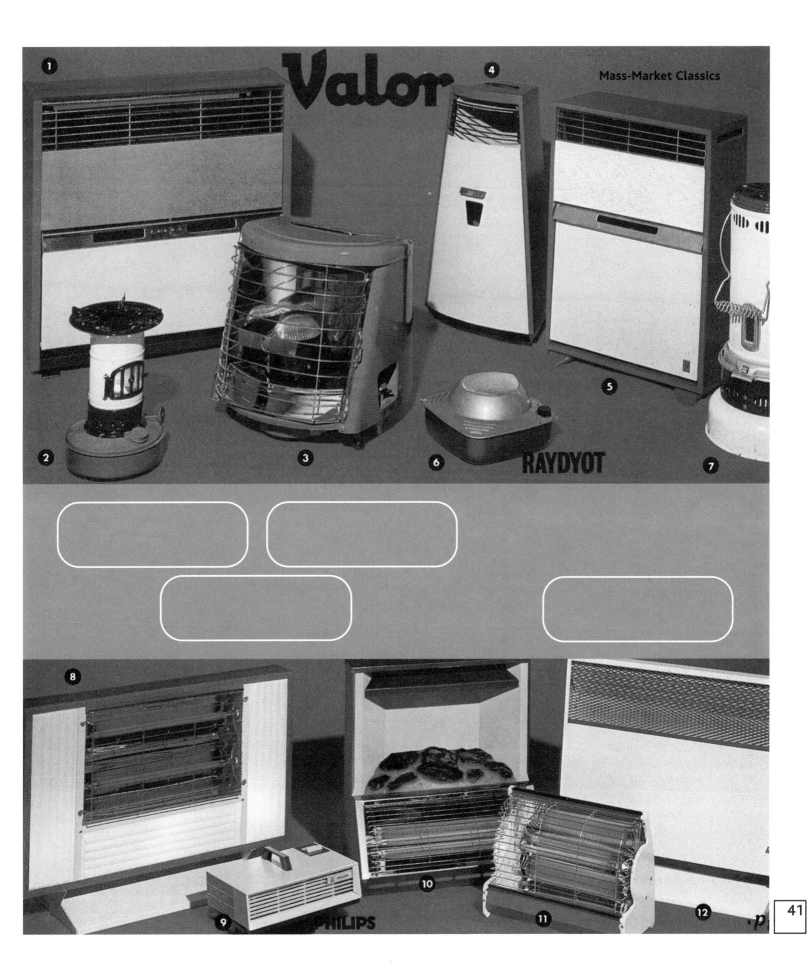

For immediate comfort

Modern living needs modern methods of heating. A Ferranti electric fire presents a design best suited to provide immediate comfort and make the fullest use of power. The reflector is shaped and the element positioned to throw out the widest zone of warmth in which the ideal living temperature is maintained.

Since the heat is immediately effective and warms by direct radiation no loss results from a proper flow of fresh air in the room.

The construction of a Ferranti fire ensures that you will have a permanent heating unit of the highest efficiency in your home.

FERRANTI LIMITED MOSTON MANCHESTER 10

Less grand but equally ubiquitous is the three-bar electric heater. According to a British local government website promoting the 'wise use of electricity', the electric bar heater is an expensive and inefficient way to heat the home. While I care about energy efficiency, I don't think they have taken into account its versatility and multi-functionality. An electric bar heater can save on buying and running other household appliances; also available in single-bar or two-bar versions, this powerful little heater is equally as adept at cooking toast, marshmallows and tinned sausages. It is at ease in singeing the fur of pets, or giving unattended toddlers a means to burn the house down.

The sheer pleasure of its affordability, coupled with almost instant heat, coerced designers into coming up with non-topple versions like the Windsor. Still highly sought after by impoverished students in the UK, this simple piece of design is very much an icon and still available from a car boot sale near you.

It spawned a surprisingly legal wall-mounted bathroom heater favoured by cold-blooded pensioners and manufactured by Dimplex, and the Space Age ceiling-mounted Thermair and Valor models.

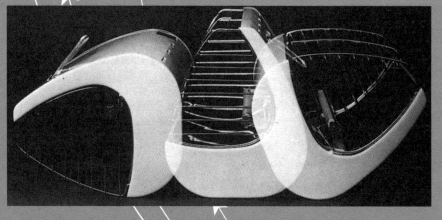

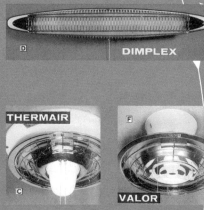

Top, a shiny two-bar heater from Ferranti

Above, rock and roll: a self-righting electric heater

Right, wall and ceiling mounted heaters from Dimplex, Thermair and Valor, from the UK's Freemans catalogue 1969

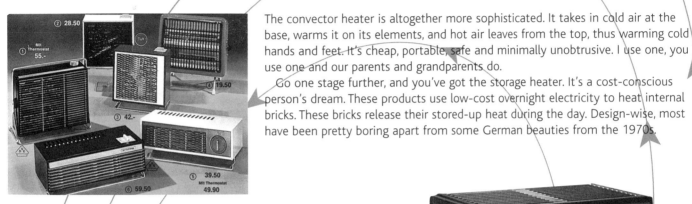

The convector heater is altogether more sophisticated. It takes in cold air at the base, warms it on its elements, and hot air leaves from the top, thus warming cold hands and feet. It's cheap, portable, safe and minimally unobtrusive. I use one, you use one and our parents and grandparents do.

Go one stage further, and you've got the storage heater. It's a cost-conscious person's dream. These products use low-cost overnight electricity to heat internal bricks. These bricks release their stored-up heat during the day. Design-wise, most have been pretty boring apart from some German beauties from the 1970s.

Clockwise from above, a collection of electric heaters from Quelle, 1971; 1960s pop geometry applied to storage heaters from Germany; German storage heaters, which otherwise are pretty boring; you could even buy timber-effect storage heaters to blend in with your decor

43

The bedroom

What are bedrooms for, apart from sleeping and having the odd bit of rumpy-pumpy? As long as the bed is comfortable, what more do you need? The answer is classic design. What bedroom is complete without scratchy, porn-style wicker furniture, teasmade, trouser press and fitted wardrobe with satin-padded hangers? It would be cruel to introduce children to a world without bunk beds in the shape of a double-decker London bus, and it would be doubly cruel to deny them sleep-overs and the use of Holly Hobbie slumberbags.

Wardrobes

I am a great fan of the fitted wardrobe. A bedroom is not complete without a wall-to-wall line of cupboards, drawers and storage units containing colour-coordinated separates on padded satin hangers. Pretty bags of potpourri nestling among neatly-folded smalls and shoes lined on high-rise shoe apartment contraptions (ranked according to width at the toe or heel height).

The really forward-thinking wardrobe specialist may go as far as building a dressing table into the wardrobe ensemble, or incorporating a wardrobe door that opens to reveal a drop-down bed. One resourceful designer confused matters by making the bed as a divan in the same material and colour as the wardrobe, resulting in what is in fact a bedrobe (not to be confused with that useful item of attire, the dressing gown).

For those of temporary abode or wall-to-wall unbelievers, there is always the zip up 'z-bed of the storage world' wardrobe. A bedsit favourite, these are hollow tubular steel beauties covered in what look like tablecloths from a transport cafe and accessed by zips.

E £129.50

G £229.99

From top, a coordinated ensemble from Marshall Ward, UK, 1986, ideal for bedroom farces; bed and storage in one, from Littlewoods, 1986; the same UK retailer also combined bed with wardrobe, desk and shelving

Opposite page, clockwise from top, a collection of brightly coloured storage accessories including the obligatory padded satin hanger from Canadian catalogue Montgomery Ward, 1968; masses of storage for shoes and suits from Neckermann, 1979; patterned wardrobe covers from German catalogue Schwab, 1971

01

02

57

H

J

K

L

M

N

white

white

81

45

T

U

P

Mehrzweckschrank
49,90

Schrank
119,—

Schrank
ab 64,90

Wäscheboy
17,90

Schrank
ab 64,90

90

K

DB

DB

L

47

Dressing tables

This is a girl thing. The idea of a dressing table is like that of a thespian preparing to go on stage. A lady sits at a dressing table preparing herself for her exacting day or night ahead.

The perfect dressing table should be not dissimilar to a Liberace piano: ornate, gold-leafed and with a mirror surrounded by bulbs. It must, be complemented by a pink poodle seat.

If the lady is preparing to make a glamour statement, then her dressing table has to complement that ambition and the seat should be her metaphorical throne.

The Europeans tried to go all modernist with flip-up mirrors, veneers and spindly legs, while Habitat did the built-in thing with its Summa range. I wouldn't want my wife going down any other route than the glam option.

Clockwise from top left, dressing table with curtains, from UK catalogue Brian Mills, 1979; European modernism from Neckermann, 1969; pink poodle stool from Sears, 1963; a built-in wardrobe/dressing table – the perfect place to prepare for a night out; Liberace style

Teasmades

I hate tea, cannot stand the smell of it on people's breath, claim to be useless at making it, and have never owned a teapot. However, for those who do enjoy this brown, watery substance, I can understand the success of a device that wakes them up with a hot cup of their morning tipple. It's hard to understand why a gadget that has been in mass production since 1930 has become an item of irony, kitsch and often ridicule. How many inventions first registered in 1902 are still sold using ostensibly the same technology more than a century later?

Left, the Goblin teasmade from the late 1970s, for that perfect morning cuppa

Below, a vintage model from the 1950s with beautiful styling

A brief history of teasmades

1902: Londoner Frank Clarke patented 'An apparatus whereby a cup of tea or coffee is automatically made'

1932: R Grumble of Eltham, London, made an automatic teasmade incorporating a Crown Derby teapot

1933: First mass-produced teasmade, the Goblin D20

1994: Some 50 models later, Goblin released The Radio Teamatic 10610R, a radio/teasmade/clock combo

2002: The teasmade of today is the Swan D01P1

Duvets, headboards and divans

I didn't experience duvets till my teens. Luxury had always been nylon or, in winter, winceyette sheets. But when duvets, or continental quilts as we called them, invaded the British Isles, we didn't put barbed wire back on our beaches.

Instead we welcomed them with open arms, in all their wonderfully named 'tog value' forms. It was this new word 'tog', and the fact that 'tog-value' (the measure of insulation performance of a duvet, which for the scientifically-minded is equal to ten times the temperature difference between the two sides of a duvet, measured in degrees Celsius) was measured by a 'togometer', cemented the duvet in my heart. I'm a sucker for silly names.

Duvets revolutionised making the bed. No more lifting the mattress and tucking sheets and covers in, no more folding over the top sheet. Although I have still not mastered the art of changing the duvet cover, I can spot a good duvet cover design. Duvets became a canvas for popular culture, from Playboy to Dirty Dancing.

In Britain, the king of all king-size duvets was Coloroll. The 1980s aesthetic for teenage boys' bedrooms everywhere – graphic red, grey, white and black combinations – was wonderfully exploited by this manufacturer.

From top, *1980s diagonal from Littlewoods, 1986; Playboy glamour for suburban homes; togs are us; retailer Burlington's take on Playboy, 1993; a bed to make sweet music in from Sears, 1981*

Opposite page, Dirty Dancing in the bedroom

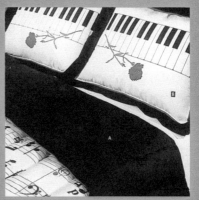

For those of you who haven't experienced the divan, and insist on a sleek-lined bed with legs, then you must have too much space in your house, or perhaps you have a dearth of possessions, are unclean and have no change of bedding?

A divan is simply a bed with drawers underneath. I know that empty space can be used for storage, but I like my contraceptives, wet wipes and flat lemonade to be in a handy drawer.

The mother of all divans is the Bedivan, a divan whose drawer opens to reveal a second bed. Crafty stuff. The Rolls Royce of divans is the Colonial Bookcase Captain's Bed, which allows you to sleep on a whole lifetime's possessions. Unless you are a very heavy sleeper, or as drunk as a lord, no-one is going to rob you while you sleep.

Above, There's no wasted space in this divan from Germany's Schopflin catalogue, 1978

Opposite page, who needs sheets or a duvet when you can show off your patterned mattress?

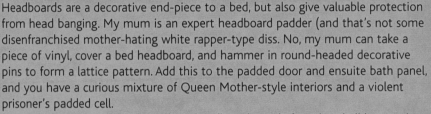

Headboards are a decorative end-piece to a bed, but also give valuable protection from head banging. My mum is an expert headboard padder (and that's not some disenfranchised mother-hating white rapper-type diss. No, my mum can take a piece of vinyl, cover a bed headboard, and hammer in round-headed decorative pins to form a lattice pattern. Add this to the padded door and ensuite bath panel, and you have a curious mixture of Queen Mother-style interiors and a violent prisoner's padded cell.

Headboard decoration ranges from headboards made from baseball bats and national flags (in case you wake up not sure which country you are in) to lily pad-shaped boards and trompe l'oeil.

In the 1970s you could judge a modernist by his or her headboard. Gadget freaks and playboys demanded their headboards contained alarms, fridges and integral music centres with headphones. Was this to shut out the moaning?

Above and opposite page, headboards in every shape and size – but preferably padded. From the catalogue of UK retailer Brian Mills, 1979

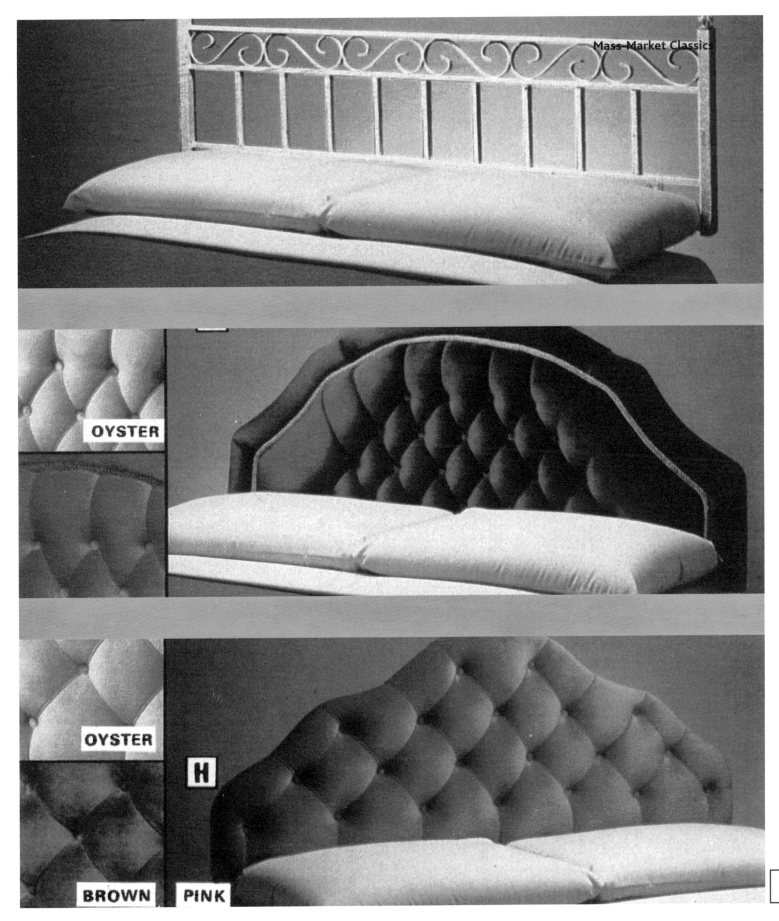

OYSTER

OYSTER

H

BROWN PINK

Kids' stuff: cots, bunk beds and futons

The kids' bedroom has long been a challenge for bed designers (has anyone ever met a bed designer?. Whoever these designers are, they have risen to the task). Babies and toddlers are delicate things and need to be protected, and while the traditional cot does look like a cage for dangerous animals, it is a design that prevents them from falling out of bed, biting visitors or strangling the dog. The bars also make good grips for learning to stand or imitating King Kong.

As the little one grows out of their cot, and the social services force you to release it from the cage, it would be cruel if they weren't allowed to sleep in a polypropylene replica of a Ferrari F1 car or plywood model of the Space Shuttle.

When the second 'surprise' comes along, it's time to invest in bunk beds and enjoy the sibling scraps over who sleeps on the top bunk.

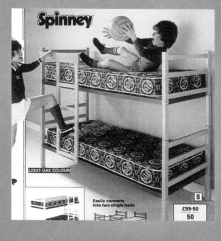

Clockwise from top, safety first for kids, from Eatons, 1970; some bunks were sophisticated play areas; while less privileged children had to make do with simple models; bunk beds from Marshall Ward, 1986; boys with more parental sponsorship got beds in the shape of racing cars

Opposite page, build-your-own-bed, from UK Homemaker magazine, 1967

WIN A £360 CARAVAN

BUNKS YOU CAN BUILD

EXTRA!

20 PAGE
SUPPLEMENT ON
SPACE SAVING

FABULOUS
BARGAIN
9-IN-1 TOOL
FOR 10s 3d

Next come sleep-overs, and that's an excuse to buy slumberbags. Just don't tell the kids they're just sleeping bags with matching pillows. As with duvets, the slumberbag cover designs range from the sublime to the ridiculous.

When they become teenagers and start to live, thank God, entirely in their bedrooms, you can buy them a futon and get your own back for all those uncomfortable nights they have given you over the years. The Japanese, who invented the futon, have always had a penchant for self harm, embodied famously in sleeping on futons and to a lesser extent by kamikaze pilots.

mforters that convert
ags with built-in pillow

etate and 20% nylon brushed tricot.
n/Hollofill 808* polyester. Comforter
r constructed of triple layer of polyes-
pillow for slumber bag. Stitched cover
lumping of fill.
pper zips comforter into a standard-
er decorative print or solid side out.
s or when children's friends sleep over.
rm water and tumble dry.
r measures 68x80 inches fitting a twin-
r bag measures 34x80 inches.
INFORMATION:
®†. Shpg. wt. 3 lbs. $24.99
*King®**. Shpg. wt. 3 lbs. 24.99
*Jack®††. Shpg. wt. 3 lbs. 24.99
ke. Shpg. wt. 3 lbs. 24.99
Skate. Shpg. wt. 3 lbs. 24.99

e the look . . . . see page 1357.

†®Trademark of Binney and Smith Inc.
ration   ††®Trademark of Borden, Inc.

(G thru L)
Your choice
$24.99

Right, selection of children's bedding, from Snoopy through to a pencil case

Opposite page, slumberbags – sleeping bags with matching pillows – ideal for sleep-over parties

The z-bed

What a truly fantastic invention the z-bed is. Cheap and convenient, they fold up to fit in a cupboard or under a bed. They are also magnificently uncomfortable, guaranteed to prevent mother-in-laws from outstaying their welcome, and noisy enough to warn you of any monkey-business going on during teenage sleep-overs.

With brand names like Stowaway, and the relatively upmarket Rollaway with built-in wheels, they do exactly what they say. And with space at a premium, they are ripe for a bit of 21st century modernisation.

Z-beds seemed to reach the current nadir of their evolutionary state in the late 1970s with a double-decker, double z-bed version and the extremely crafty flat z-bed that was so slender it could be stored in a couple of inches of space behind a wardrobe.

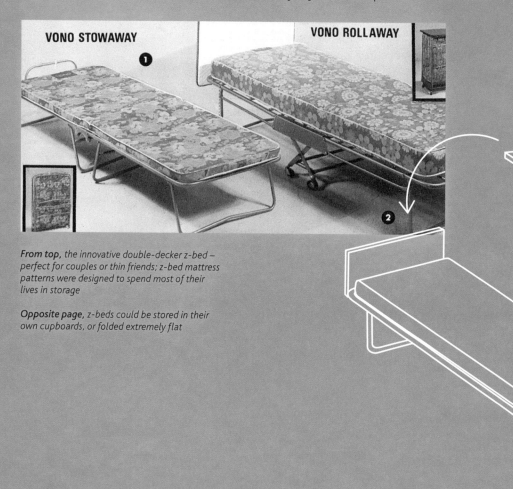

From top, the innovative double-decker z-bed – perfect for couples or thin friends; z-bed mattress patterns were designed to spend most of their lives in storage

Opposite page, z-beds could be stored in their own cupboards, or folded extremely flat

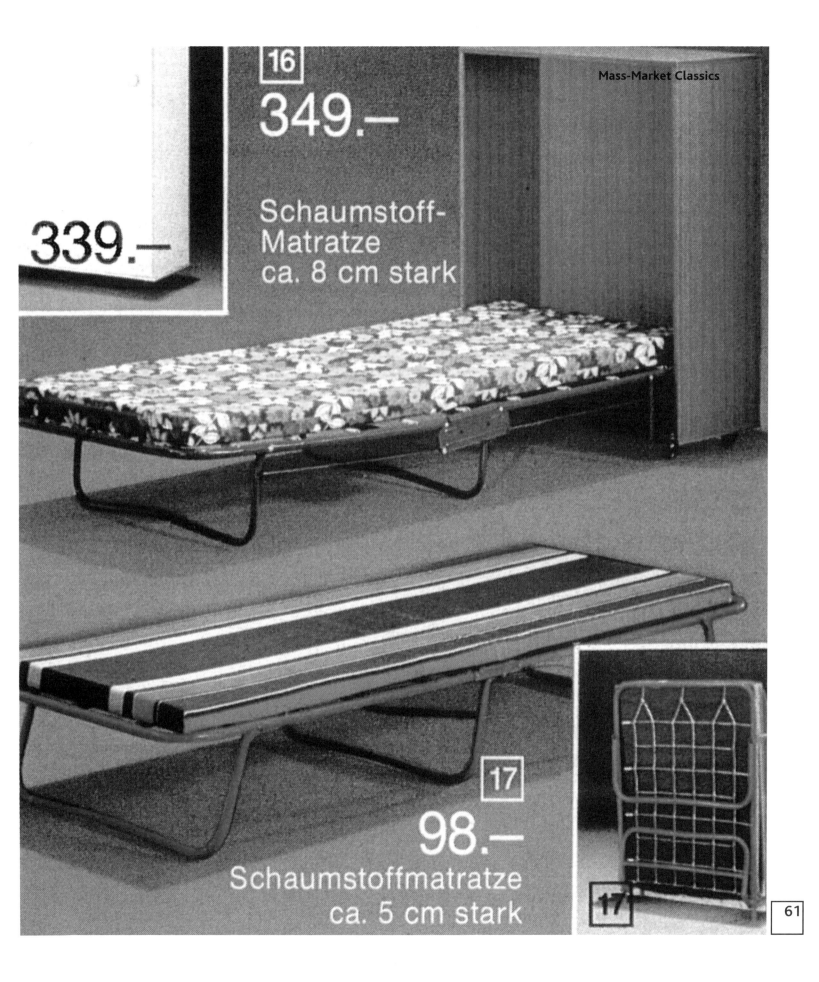

16

349.—

339.—

Schaumstoff-
Matratze
ca. 8 cm stark

17

98.—

Schaumstoffmatratze
ca. 5 cm stark

Rocking chairs

Quite why a chair only suitable for senility, or those with seasickness fetishes should have sold so well is anyone's guess. Maybe the purchasers don't know either, as most are relegated to remote corners or to rust on the veranda.

Some scholars attribute rocking chairs to Egyptian pharaohs, others to the Greeks, while Americans claim they were invented by J Andrew Smith of Texas.

Rocking chairs conjure up frightening images of Welsh women in silly black hats and lace shawls trying to spin wool while rocking gently back and forth. Or of crazy American pensioners rocking violently on their rickety chairs, dreaming of capturing and torturing a lone walker.

The classic rocking chair has to be the dark wood, spindled-arm kitsch model, now available once again from Habitat. The one modernist rocker that approached mass success was the RAR Rocker by Eames, which stood out in the 1950s from a plethora of designer rocking chairs by Gio Ponti, Piero Fornasetti *et al*. More recently, British designer Ron Arad has attempted to inject a new feeling of cool into rocking chairs with a special version of his Tom Vac chair for Vitra.

Above, *the classic rocking chair, from Habitat, 1977. It has recently been reissued*

Right, *country style and with their own valances, these rocking rockers date from 1968*

Opposite page, *although designers have recently tried to reinvent rocking chairs with glamour, this design remains the standard*

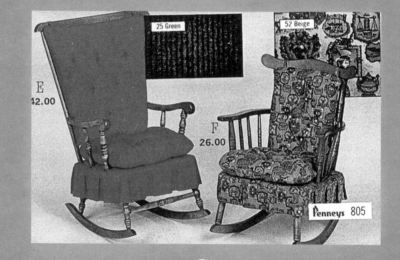

Net curtains

I have got a thing against net curtains. It seems pointless having windows if you are going to shut out the world. But this book is a celebration of popular design, and there are few things more popular than net curtains. They go beyond privacy and are used as decoration by the design-challenged or those possessing a larger dose of irony than yours truly. Whether they are plain, broderie anglaise, floral lace or printed, I don't like them. But they are worth a few pages in this book.

Above and opposite page, nets, nets and more nets. They may provide discretion for curtain twitchers and keen Neighbourhood Watchers, but that's no excuse for some of these designs

Raff-
rosette,
S. 641,
Abb. 19

⑤ Raffgardine Querbehang
ab **59.-** Meter **8.90**

⑥ Volant-Store-Meterware,
auch für Blumenfenster
ab **16.90**
Auch Fertig-Stores

The bathroom

This is a room with a door that locks. It is where we get rid of our waste and get clean. Most importantly, it's a sanctuary – a place to relax and soak in the bath, to sing in the shower or to catch up on your reading during an extended sit on the 'throne'. It offers a few minutes of privacy and quiet. The bathroom has not traditionally been a room of high design but some mass-market classics have been produced especially for the 'smallest room' in the house.

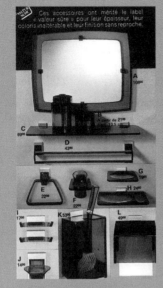

Moulded splashback storage

While design aficionados revere the moulded plastic wall storage unit 'The Utensilo' by Dorothee Maurer-Becker – have you ever tried cleaning toothbrush dribble out of one of these? – the public bought mass-market versions made by the likes of manufacturer Flair. In all their peach, avocado and pistachio glory, they had receptacles for everything from Brut 33 aftershave and Charlie perfume to dentures. The late 1970s NL 696 storage bar, which cost a cool £12.75 (or 20 weeks at 64p) from UK mail order catalogue Brian Mills, was a design classic.

However, the most useful were the bath accessory mouldings which could be bought as add-ons to your new bathroom suite and craftily double up as splashback/storage combos.

The French, as usual, had their version in brown smoked Perspex, complete with a matching ashtray to house their Gauloises next to their smoker's toothpaste.

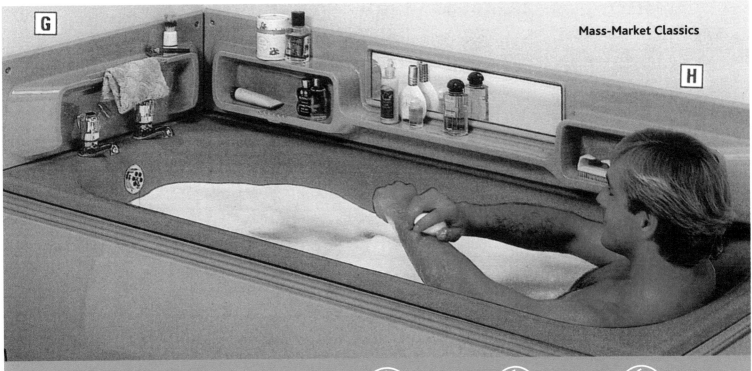

G

H

Above and below, his and hers moulded splashback storage, Brian Mills catalogue, UK, 1982

Opposite page, clockwise from top, *smoked Perspex from French retailer La Redoute; a more modest mirror/storage combo; selection of storage ideas from Brian Mills, 1982; exotic mouldings from Schwab, 1974; bathroom from Freemans catalogue, UK ,1973*

K

M

Ali Babas

Who would have thought that a sneaky wicker basket, which provided a cunning hiding place in *Ali Baba and the Forty Thieves*, would become an icon of the home? As a small child, our Ali Baba was my favourite hide-and-seek bolt hole, from where I would suddenly appear in an attempt to frighten my mum. She in turn would feign a surprise of heart attack proportions.

The Ali Baba brings a bit of the exotic East to the bathroom, and is eminently sensible in allowing dirty laundry to breathe, helping to negate musty smells.

From top, a taste of eastern promise, Ali Babas are also kind to clothes; modern-style Ali Babas in a range of colours, from Sears, 1984; Ali Babas come in a range of sizes and make ideal hiding places for children or snakes

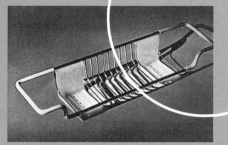

The adjustable bath rack

When it comes to bath racks, the purist may fondly remember the plastic moulded bargain basement-style version. Cheap it may be, but this fine invention makes the bath-time experience that much simpler, in terms of access to soap, loofahs and rubber ducks. It became a true classic in its extendable form.

Designed by Peter Bell for Valbania in 1950, you can simply extend the non-slip handle by sliding it along the chrome arms, and you have a bath rack that fits most widths.

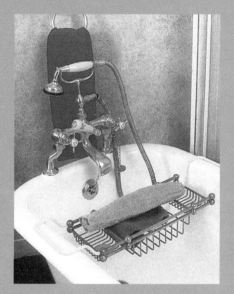

Clockwise from top, the iconic rack from Valbania, designed by Peter Bell; plastic given a heritage feel with floral transfers; the Valbania rack works in both traditional and modern settings, and can adjust to a range of widths

Three-piece pedestal sets

Bathroom fact 1: Men often have a problem with aim when emptying their bladders.
Solution: A washable bit of carpet that fits around the toilet pedestal.

Bathroom fact 2: When you get out of the bath, wet feet turn hard floors into a slip hazard, or ruin a fitted carpet with all that dripping water.
Solution: A bath mat that matches the mat around the toilet pedestal.

Bathroom fact 3: When you retire to the bathroom to read the daily paper, the toilet seat can be hard on your rear.
Solution: A cover to fit the toilet seat that matches the mat around the pedestal of the toilet and the bath mat.

Name a fashion and there has been a pedestal set marketed to complement it. From pink shag pile, through butterfly-embroidered brown wool to ocelot and jaguar prints, they have all appeared on toilet seats and on the bathroom floor.

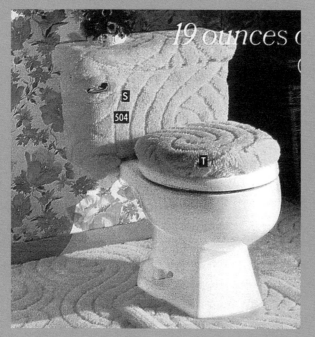

From top, pedestal sets lend extra cosiness to a bathroom. This example is from the Marshall Ward catalogue, 1986; bright colours brought pop design into suburban bathrooms; why stop at just the toilet seat? Cisterns could be upholstered too

Opposite page, for the ultimate in coordinated interiors, embroidered pedestal sets were available

B

C

G

E

D

596

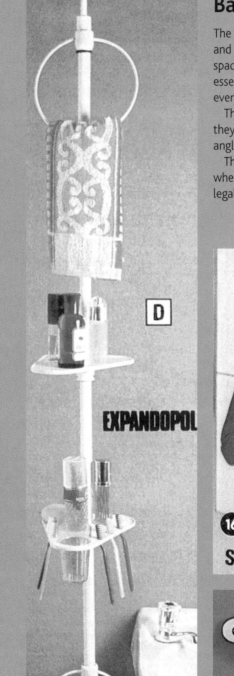

Bathroom gizmos

The bathroom may be one of the smallest rooms, but it houses many cabinets and gadgets. And it certainly houses more wet socks, so the 18 metres of drying space gained by pulling your Tidy Dry, Tidy Two, or Tidy Line over your bath was essential. The Expandopole, £8 in the UK, was a 1977 design classic that held everything you could want an expanding bathroom pole to hold, and some.

The 'under-sink-pull-out-short-persons-step', meanwhile, is ideal for kids so they can pull faces in the Self-Stik mirror tile (which could be positioned at crazy angles to great effect) while polishing their pearlies.

Then there are the roof-mounted heater/light fittings, which I will have fitted when I become a pensioner, even if my bathroom is warm enough, just so I can legally get a dangerous-looking heater into my bathroom.

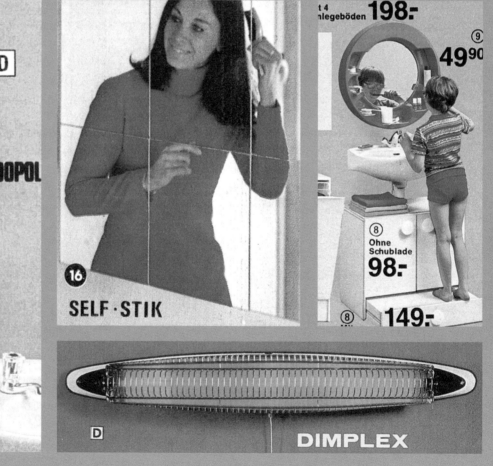

624

TIDY-TWO

A

DRYING SPACE: 25 ft

B

DRYING SPACE: 40 ft

DRYING SPACE: 60 ft

TIDY-DRY

C

TIDY-TWO
TIDY-LINE
TIDY-DRY

Above, a selection of Tidy clothes-drying products sold through the Freemans catalogue, UK, 1962

Opposite page, Expandopoles, Self-Stik mirrors, bathroom cabinets with built-in steps for kids and wall-mounted heaters: the bathroom was a hive of product innovation

The kitchen and dining room

In between building wall units and decorating headboards, TV domestic heroes implore us to create perfect eat-live spaces. The kitchen consumer porn brigade has turned to design as a way of wrestling money from our wallets. That easiest of targets, Alessi's Philippe Starck lemon squeezer, may look modern in a kitsch way, but give me a basic squeezer from Woolworths any day. Even down to the humble stirring implement, simple is best – a wooden spatula won't burn your tongue like stainless steel.

Fitted kitchens

I love fitted kitchens. All that wall-to-wall storage and those corner unit carousels encourage all but the most dedicated country cottage-lover to hide away their strings of onions, ladles and kettles. While the made-to-measure suit declined in popularity, the bespoke tradition went from strength to strength in the kitchen. Having the local fitted kitchen specialist round to measure up your kitchen became the equivalent of a trip to Savile Row. A visit to the showroom to see the plan was like the first fit of the suit, with minor adjustments to be made. The filling of the cupboards was the pre-night out trying-on, and the first meal cooked in the kitchen was a big night out in the new 'irresistible to the ladies' outfit.

Once the Second World War was over, there was reduced demand for designers to make space in tanks, submarines and bomb shelters, and it seems that many must have turned their hands to kitchen cupboards and drawers that turn into mini tables, chopping boards, serving trolleys and rubbish bins.

Clockwise from top, the fitted kitchen was not only the domain of women; all kitchen functions could fit into the smallest area; fitted kitchens came hand-in-hand with open plan living; the kitchen could reflect your 1970s clothing colour palette; all those labour-saving devices meant the lady of the house could put her feet up

Opposite page, making the most of a small space

Breakfast bars

Long before Kellogg's came up with the idea of sticking our favourite breakfast cereals together with some kind of milk-based glue to create a breakfast bar, those folks too busy to eat at home had another kind of time-saving invention boasting the same name.

The breakfast bar was based on the idea of sitting at the bar of a hostelry serving alcohol on a high chair, except that at this bar you ate a full English breakfast, cereal and toast rather than peanuts and pork scratchings. The time-saving element came from not having to carry the food and utensils to the dining room, resulting in a welcome extra 45 seconds in bed.

From top, open-plan dining gave a feeling of space; the breakfast bar was inspired by bars in hostelries that served alcohol; with no need to carry food through to the dining room, you could spend longer in bed

Opposite page, a kitchen/bar combo from 1956

The space-saving kitchen

The concept of dining in the kitchen, where space is at a premium, has long inspired furniture designers. While not exactly up there with Louis Pasteur or Alexander Graham Bell, whoever invented the drop-leaf table should be feted for giving us space in the kitchen.

Space-saving concepts in kitchen dining also extended to the seating. The kitchen proved another fertile area for stacking and folding chairs (which thus far had their spiritual home in dowdy classrooms and dusty church halls). Now that they had entered the bright kitchens of the 1950s home, they could throw off their utilitarian plywood personas and embrace pattern and colour. And embrace it they did. Taking their lead from the interiors of US diners, kitchens became full of vinyl-covered stacking chairs with spindly chrome legs, arranged around melamine-coated, drop-leaf tables.

My house had a fantastic table with a print of fruits and vegetables on the top, inspiring thoughts of more exotic things while we ate our fish fingers.

From top, cute diner style from Graves, UK, 1974; drop-leaf tables provide extra flexibility; stacking chairs and stools are great space-savers

Opposite page, multifunctional chairs and stools added to the versatility of kitchen furniture

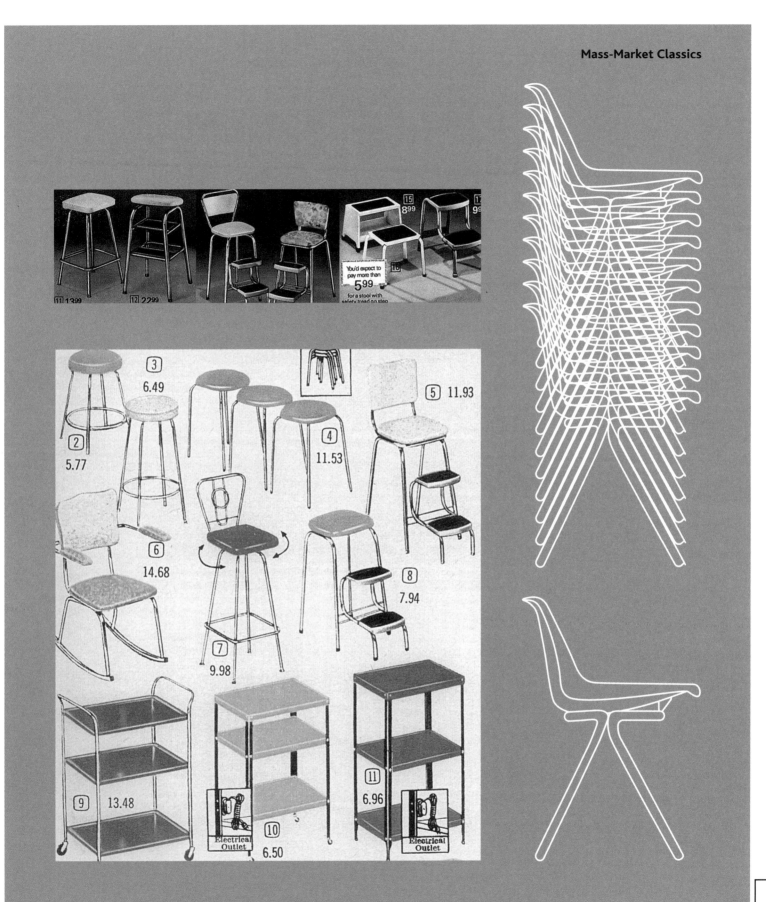

As vinyl became passé, plastic and later Perspex took over. That eminently sensible concept of wipe-clean, however, was retained. Designers were obviously inspired by the idea of practicality in the kitchen, as they churned out stools that doubled up as stepladders, and one of my all-time favourite pieces, the Pop Top stool. The Pop Top was a fine example of American home-shopping genius, a $20 round stool that had replaceable seat covers that looked like – and flipped off and on like – the caps of drink bottles. What is more, they were printed with the logos of Budweiser, Pepsi, 7-Up and the like. How cool is that, and when are they going to be brought back?

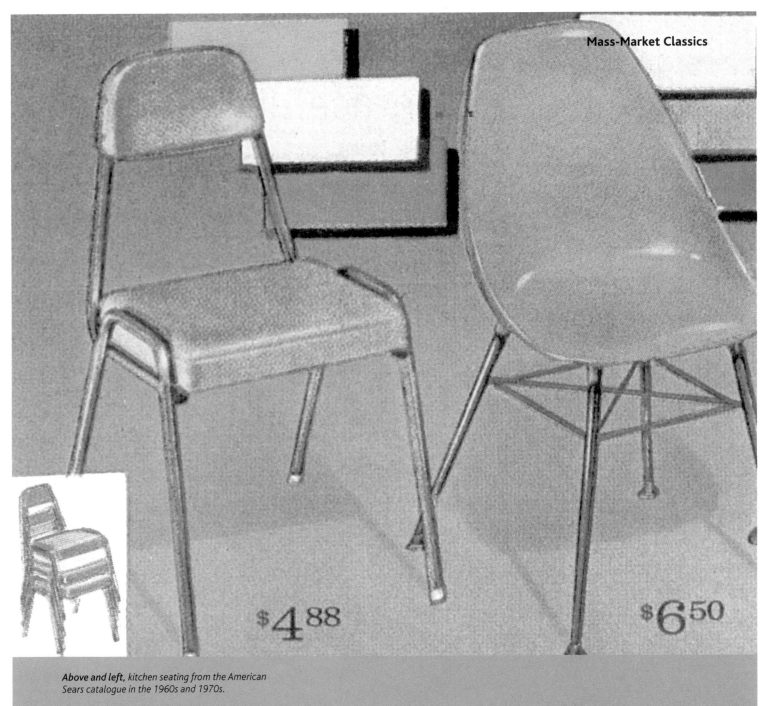

$4^{88}

$6^{50}

Above and left, *kitchen seating from the American Sears catalogue in the 1960s and 1970s.*

Opposite page, far left, *the Pop Top stool is ripe for revival*

A simple equation:

Everyone eats

+

Everyone likes to sit down

+

It's easier to eat on a level surface

=

Dining room tables and chairs

Dining tables and chairs

The equation on the left shows a functional bit of design science that has led to a functional household essential. From the tubular steel of the German Bauhaus design school, through the mid-century utility of Robin Day's veneered dining chair for London County Council, and his ply-back and steel-framed stacking chair for UK manufacturer Hille, to Eero Saarinen's pedestal chair for Knoll, the Eames-designed wire chairs from Herman Miller and the simplicity of Arne Jacobsen's Ant Chair, our dining chairs have always made a functional modern statement.

While all these famous designers produced chairs that weren't prohibitively expensive, the high street and home shopping catalogues took inspiration from them and made cool dining room sets extremely affordable.

The polished chrome spider stools with vinyl seats arranged around a melamine-finish round table became a 2.2 children family staple (I don't know where the 0.2 of a child would sit, though).

In my house we had Taranto brown polypropylene and chrome chairs with a rectangular teak-coloured table that could fit a couple of guests at a squeeze.

On the other side of the Atlantic, grey smoked-Plexiglas replaced the 'diner' style of the 1950s.

Clockwise from top, futuristic plastic and chrome; 1950s dining chair by Robin Day; democratic dining sets

Opposite page, a vision of dining elegance from Habitat, 1974

88

France, with its fashion for futurism, took to the white melamine, Saarinen-inspired pod-like dining set. Habitat took their cue from Charles Eames with the still sought-after Bertoia wire chair and round oak-veneered table with polished aluminium pedestal.

The Bauhaus cane and chrome chair teamed with a chrome-legged dark wood table was a staple at Habitat through the 1970s and into the 1980s. The less said about the Larry laminated chipboard table and epoxy-coated matching folding chairs the better, but they sold like hot cakes during the early 1980s. While few Hollywood directors would eat their dinner off them, director-style furniture became an affordable, and at the time cosmopolitan, dining option.

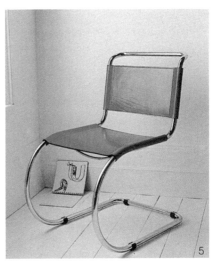

From top, Pernnial 1970s favourites –
*Bauhaus-inspired cane and chrome chairs
with chrome-legged table; ubiquitous folding
bum-numbers; 1950s white pedestal chairs from
La Redoute, a 1970s Bauhaus copy from Habitat*

*Left and opposite page, director's chairs were big
with film fans in the 1980s*

Pendant lights

If, like me, you don't enjoy eating in half-light, and want to make sure there aren't any bits of celery in the sauce, then a pendant light over the dining room table is a godsend. By far the most popular of all time is the round Japanese lantern. When they first became popular in the UK in the early 1970s they cost £1; a decade later they were still £1.50. Those with cash to spend went for a rise-and-fall unit, enabling hosts to impress guests by bringing the light down to hover, rather like a spacecraft, just above the table. With the light in its 'fall' position, there was no hiding place for vegetables. Fruit lovers, meanwhile, had to be careful not to eat the US Fruit lamps.

Clockwise from top, a 1960s mushroom pendant; the Japanese-style paper lampshade was cheap and ubiquitous; pendants could be lowered to highlight casserole contents

Opposite page, the pendant was an integral part of any groovy interior

Common chairs

Some people have a chair fetish. They bid over £1,000 for a Mies van der Rohe or an Eames on Ebay. There's no doubting that the design of a chair is important but it's stating the blooming obvious to remind design freaks that chairs are for sitting on. It is for their function that we buy chairs and that is why so many designers constantly strive to design the perfect seat.

It seems like a cliché to talk about the Bauhaus, but when Walter Gropius set up the Bauhaus design school it was with mass production in mind.

Among the thousands of chairs, the master of the mass market, the Polyprop stacking chair by Hille, designed by Robin Day. First produced in 1962, more than 14 million have been sold, and 500,000 are still produced each year. I remember them giving me a 'dead' bottom at school. We also had a bright orange and chrome stack in the corner of our living room which would be unstacked when more than one guest arrived. They became ubiquitous – the inspiration for designers the world over.

Other big names also produced affordable chairs: Eero Saarinen's pedestal Tulip by Knoll is a classic; the Diamond steel mesh Bertoia chair also from Knoll is seen at auction even though they are still made today, and the Arne Jacobsen Ant chair, manufactured by Fritz Hansen, can be seen in bars and bistros the world over.

Top five chairs

In at five, Habitat's Taranto

At four it's cane and chrome by Bauhaus, Habitat 1970s

Straight in at three, Arne Jacobsen's Ant Chair, 1951

At two, it's Bertoia's metal Diamond chair, 1952

Top of the chair pops is by rocking Robin Day. It's his Polyprop stacker on the Hille label, 1962

Opposite page from top, the classic Bertoia chair; Arne Jacobsen's Ant chair

Below, clockwise from top, Robin Day's polypropylene stackers for Hille, the U22 chair, and Saarinen's 1950s Tulip pedestal; these bentwood chairs came in a variety of colours and were popular in the 1970s; the Polyprop came in many guises

Cocktail bars

Who needs to go out to eat when we've got celebrity chefs sharing their wisdom and cheesy one-liners on TV, and supermarkets sell shrink-wrapped haute cuisine? And why go to the pub when you can sit on your own bar stool at your very own bar?

Mail order catalogues sold us a little piece of the pub throughout the latter half of the 20th century. The finest example of the home pub must be that developed by Wards Barrel furniture in the late 1960s. It was made from 'barrels used to age fine bourbon, but which by law are used only once'. Bound with metal hoops and clad with cushioned vinyl, these proved the ideal receptacle for tankards and bowls of nuts. They were also a great excuse to get your wife into an off-the-shoulder top, just like the wench at your local.

The 1960s modernist who wanted his or her dining room bar to match their padded bed headboards and bathroom doors, chose their diamond-patterned chrome-studded, walnut-woodgrain vinyl topped bar. These brought that 'pick-up' bar ethic to suburban homes.

The home bartender in Europe chose to relive evenings spent in Fred's Football Bar in Torremolinos. Their bars proved a great place to house the sherry decanter, felt bulls, maracas, castanets and straw donkeys. The cruise-aspiring Brits, who liked to imagine they were Queen Elizabeth on tour, favoured the Boat Bar, filling it with dolls of the Commonwealth,

cocktail shakers, jars of cherries and Babycham glasses crammed with umbrella cocktail sticks.

In the 1980s, home bars became like discos in their black and chrome splendour, and bar designers got clever with the wonderfully kitsch globe on wheels that turned into a mobile bar.

Left, three bars ranging from padded leather to high-tech disco, bottom

Below, the ultimate accessory was the globe that flipped open to reveal a minibar

Opposite page, a selection from Canada's Montgomery Ward catalogue, 1970, including the infamous barrel furniture

Serving trolleys

In the rush to bring the sophistication of the restaurant dining experience into the home, design often lost its function-above-form ethic. This is nowhere more evident than in the serving trolley. Mein hostess would certainly make an entrance with a rustic trolley with so-called realistic cartwheels, which originated in Bavaria in the early 1980s. It must have been fun sitting down for dinner in your lederhosen, felt trilbies worn at a jaunty angle with feathers tucked into the brim, sounding a cow bell with one hand and holding a stein mug overflowing with German beer in the other. You would marvel at your other half coming out of the kitchen wearing her (or his?) hair in pigtails and sporting a milkmaid style dress, pushing a carved wooden Bavarian serving trolley with cart-like wheels and laden with sauerkraut and frankfurters.

Early versions were much simpler, with the aim of getting food from kitchen to dining room with the minimum of fuss. In the 1970s plastic circular ones sold by the thousand and today's Habitat version retains similar simplistic styling.

My favourite is the fold-flat version that can be stored under the stairs, but the true top-of-the-range product is a serving trolley that also warms the food. There was the mid-century serving trolley with hotplate by Alfred Cox Ltd, and a canteen on wheels that dinner party throwers of the 1970s wheeled to the table.

Above, serving trolleys were useful for storing entire dinner services – plus food. The most famous were designs by Hostess, left

Opposite page, if this image from the UK's Ideal Home magazine, in 1974, is to be believed, serving trolleys could be taken outdoors for picnics

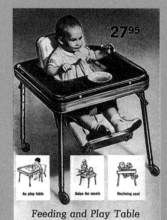

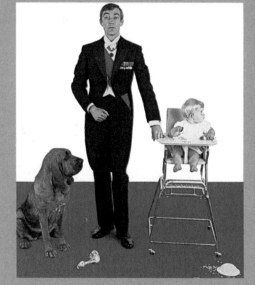

Highchairs

The mischievous masochist in me has enjoyed watching the good lady wife struggling to eat her dinner, while the youngest is on her lap dropping sloppy baby mush off his spoon onto her clothes. But it is probably best to sacrifice this fun for the mealtime peace brought about by plonking baby in a highchair.

The cleverest design was the 1960s 'Baby Relax' from the UK, that could be set up in nine different ways: a highchair with a feeding tray or a low chair, a recliner, baby seat, carry chair, potty, car seat, sun chair with canopy or a swing.

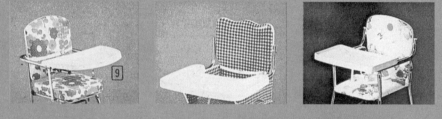

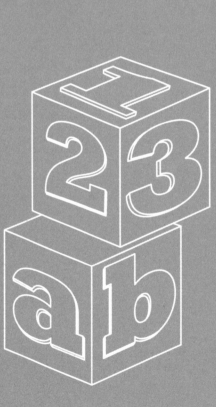

Clockwise from top left, highchairs made feeding into playtime; three gaily coloured highchairs from the 1970s; the 'Baby Relax', 1960, went way beyond the brief; highchairs on wheels allowed for comic caper potential

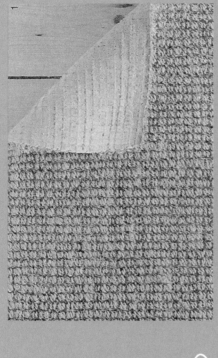

Natural flooring

I have never really understood the attraction of sisal, seagrass, jute and coir as flooring materials. Spill liquid on them and, by the morning, the seeds that fell off your seeded batch loaf will be sending up shoots. Worse still, transferring a dining table quickie onto a sisal floor is not an option unless you have a fetish for chafed backsides. It must be the result of a desire to naturally complement the Bauhaus cane-upholstered dining chairs and bamboo pendant lightshades.

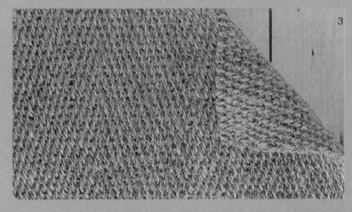

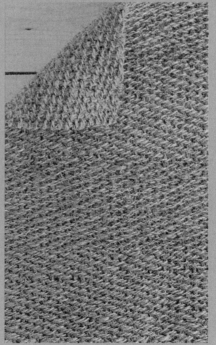

Superfresco and 'deathtrap' polystyrene ceiling tiles

Anaglypta was patented by its inventor Thomas Palmer in 1887. This cheap, cotton pulp wallcovering is embossed with shapes ranging from 1930s' Deco patterns to random lines. My mum's kitchen was clad from wall to wall in the Superfresco version. Unlike woodchip papers, you weren't stuck with the wallcovering for the next three generations

I never understood why we, and thousands like us, had polystyrene tiles on the ceiling. Maybe it was the thrilling thought of them dripping into red-hot oil during a chip-pan fire?

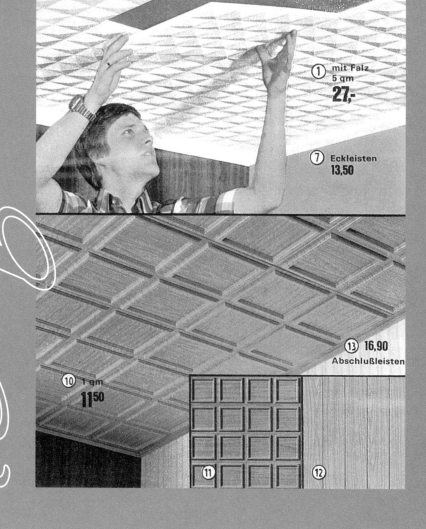

Above, *textured wall coverings, including Anaglypta and Superfresco, were an inexpensive way of adding pattern to a room*

Right and opposite page, *polystyrene ceiling tiles, sold through German retailer Schwab in 1976, were easy to install for men in moustaches*

Deckenplatten
30×30, 40×40 und 50×50 cm

1 qm **4**⁵⁰   Styroporkleber
siehe Seite 549,
5 qm **21**⁵⁰   Position 16

⑥

**Profitieren durch
Isolieren!
Styropor-
Isolierplatten,
000×500×20 mm,
mit Nut und Feder
zur fugenlosen
Verarbeitung**

9.50

Platten = 2,5 qm

⑤

**Wand- und
Deckenpaneele
aus Holz.**

**In Eiche,
Nußbaum,
Palisander
und Kiefer
Platte
ab 7.50**

④

**Universal-
Vielzweckleiter
Aus Stahlrohr
ab 105.–
Anz. 11.–
Aus Leichtmetall
ab 195.–
Anz. 20.–**

Tupperware, melamine and Pyrex

Any kitchen accessory that resulted in a party has to be a design classic. Designed by Earl Tupper in 1946, those infamous parties began in 1948 and by 1951 were so successful that Tupperware was withdrawn from stores and exclusively sold by the Tupperware Home Demonstration system.

This was a way for housewives to make money. Tupperware keeps your food fresh and prevents aromas mixing with other produce in your fridge – as well as empowering women.

If you find the originals in a charity store today, they are invariably as useful as they were when new. The satisfying 'clip' of the airtight seal, and the sheer stackability, is design to behold. So satisfying, in fact, that said empowered housewives would get their kicks holding parties to buy Tupperware long before they thought

about holding sexy underwear parties. However, I think I'd rather attend a Tupperware/sexy underwear hybrid party, as I like my functionality and cheap thrills combined.

Tupperware is only part of the story of the synthetic kitchen. Indeed it was possible to ditch crockery altogether. Melamine is an unbreakable compound used in households not wedded to china. The colours that could be achieved make it a favourite of design-savvy collectors (check out the bright orange sets). A staple of picnic sets from the 1940s onwards, I believe it is due a reappreciation.

From top, the ultimate social cachet – an invite to a Tupperware party; fantastic plastic Tupperware; Melaware is ripe for reappreciation

Opposite page, Melmex got the seal of approval in 1960s homes

Melmex in safe hands!

Pyrex is a cooking pot material that withstands oven heat (it is borosilicate glass that has a low coefficient of thermal expansion, making it heat resistant). My nan had a floral-patterned set that gradually became black with what looked like burnt gravy, but her braised steak, onion and dumpling casserole tasted all the better for it and remains firmly imprinted on my taste buds.

Right, ovenware came in a variety of patterns and colours; Pyrex clearly made the best vessels

Opposite page, the Pyrex range included cups, kettles, mixing bowls and food warmers

Pyrex facts

1. The name is derived from a nine-inch glass pie plate invented in 1913 by Dr Littleton in Germany

2. The public bought 4.5 million Pyrex items in 1919

3. Did you know you can cook on the flame with Pyrex? The clued-up have known this since Flame Pyrex was introduced in 1936

PYREX

for good looking cooking and serving

For casseroles and baking One of many generous dishes in the 'Pyrex' range for hungry families. Clear oval easy-grip casserole, 4pt. 15/4. Also 2½pt. 10/7

Very good mixers! Opal Carnival mixing bowl set–also very useful for making and serving custards, for example. Three bowls, 1pt., 1½pt. and 2½pt. Complete 29/-

For pies galore! You can see the meat, see the fruit: and cook every possible kind of pie in clear 'Pyrex' pie dishes! *Oval ⅜pt. 3/5, 1½pt. 4/5, 2pt. 6/2. Oblong : 1½pt. 5/10*

'Pyrex' for beef and ginger bread! 'Pyrex' square roaster–the family size baking and roasting dish: good for roasting, naturally, and also for country-style ginger cake, and bread pudding. 12¾" x 11" x 2¾6". 12/4

Poultry in 'Pyrex' A chicken casserole with a special top that gives covered-in roasting, a very economical and tenderizing method of cooking. 11" x 9" x 6". 20/8

Always proof in 'Pyrex' puddings The popular 1½pt. clear pudding basin –one of the most-used 'Pyrex' dishes: and only 3/11. Also: 1pt. 2/11, 2½pt. 5/2

'Pyrex' for day-long drinks! Clear 'Pyrex' tumblers–in jolly red or yellow heatproof holders: for hot drinks, and cold drinks. ½pt. tumbler 2/11, with holder 5/10

For main - dish - and - vegetables: Opal 'Harvest' junior space-saver casserole set–three matching dishes with clear covers, 1pt. 1½pt. and 1¾pt. sizes. Complete 34/5

For sausages–and party-time! Keep food warm and serve party snacks in this deep oblong 'Pyrex' 'Harvest' casserole on its candle-warmer stand. 40/8. Without stand 26/1

'Pyrex' for food preparation Smooth, clean, hygienic. Food doesn't stick to it–so much easier to wash up. Rolling pin (15") 11/1. Measuring jug, ½pt. 5/2, 1pt. 6/11

A cup of tea to every taste–in 'Pyrex'! Boil the water in this 'Pyrex' tea kettle, make the tea in it, serve the tea from it! Makes 6 cups of *really* good tea. 23/3

'Pyrex' suits every table décor The Weardale Opal oval casserole is smartly at home on every table. 2½pt. size–a 'family'-plus-guests capacity. Complete 14/-

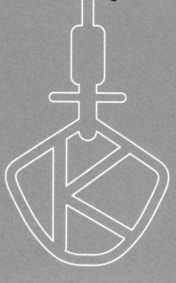

Kenwood Chefs

Kitchen gadgets come and go. There have always been bright orange, quick-buck, multipurpose vegetable peelers, slicers and scrapers — even those that turn carrots into little flower shapes — advertised alongside commemorative teaspoons in the back of Sunday paper supplements. But the Kenwood Chef with K Wheel *circa* 1978 is a mass-market design classic.

Introduced in 1948 and still a household staple, the Kenwood Chef reached design maturity in the mid-1970s with the introduction of the K Wheel, an all-singing-and-dancing kitchen wizard that liquidises, grinds coffee, extrudes sausages, peels potatoes and makes pasta — and could probably exercise the dog with a bit of tweaking.

This is multipurpose, space-saving functional design at its best and worth scouring car boots and charity shops for. The modern versions are pretty good but at £300 ($480) I think I will hold on to my trusty K Wheel.

Blender/mixer facts

1. The first blender, the 'Vibrator', was invented by Stephen J Popawski, and patented in 1922

2. The Kenwood Chef was designed by Kenneth Wood in the UK in the 1940s, well ahead of the gadget-obsessed Americans

3. 'Spin Cookery' was a US fad in the 1950s, where it became the thing to develop a whole meal based around the blender — and not just for toothless geriatrics

4. An industry war developed in the late 1950s called the 'Battle of the Buttons' (not to be confused with The Cold War, The Suez Crisis or 'Nam). The first mixers had only two buttons 'low' and 'high'. Soon there were four with 'off' and 'medium', then came 'chop', 'grate', 'dice' and 'liquefy', 'whip' and 'purée'

Right, *your meal could be as 'whizzy' as your wallpaper*

Sandwich toasters

What a brilliant invention. Compact, easy to clean, fast and foolproof, the Breville is the apogee of democratic design. I have taken my Breville through life with me. When I left home, my mum packed the Breville. I think her tears were for me (although she always enjoyed a toastie).

Morning, noon or night, in my student bedsit, the Breville churned out toasted sandwiches. They were piping hot little mammas, sealing in cheese often well past its sell-by date. The Breville even perks up even the most cardboard-like thin white sliced bread. The official Breville website says, 'Due to its moisture content, very fresh bread may not go golden brown... leave the bread out before using'.

Below, this model, the Breville, first came on to the market in 1981 and should be viewed in the same light as the iconic Hoover and Biro, which also became generic names for their product type

I thought I'd pass on a couple more tips to aid your enjoyment of the Breville

1. Don't overfill the bread; the sandwich is not elastic

2. Sliced bread that is several days old, measuring 130x110mm is ideal

3. Coat the outside of the sandwich with a thin layer of margarine

Agas and Rayburns

Agas and Rayburns are the antithesis of modern miniaturisation, and are lauded by the same people as those who swear by reproduction Chippendale furniture and captain's writing desks. They are big, and I would say ugly, cooking ranges that belong in the 18th century when they were introduced.

Yet they are as popular today in counties hellbent on nostalgia – such as the UK, the US and Canada – as they were when they were first manufactured in Sweden in 1929. In fact, the original enamel cream colour is still at the top of the list of bestsellers, but not in modernist Sweden where they have long forgotten about this design relic.

Unfortunately, the public's love of period drama means the Aga is probably here to stay, as TV churns out romanticised Aga sagas set in English country houses and cottages.

Above and opposite page, Agas and Rayburns have a cosy, country house feel

Racks of racks

Kitchen storage is an art form in itself, ranging from bread bins especially for French bread, to moulded 'tissuefoilclingfilmstringdispensers' creations and neat cleaning-cloth holders. But the iconic kitchen storage unit is the rack, and the most ubiquitous example is the wine rack. My family's tipple was beer rather than wine, so our racks of choice were for shoes, including vertical ones that held the heels towards you, see-through pocket versions, and floor-to-ceiling cloth shoe trees.

At some stage in the evolution of my family, food regained its ascendancy over shoes and our kitchen welcomed the sensible vegetable rack. Yet it is the more glamorous spice rack that brings back the most happy memories: exotically named spices such as cherry flakes, cilantro, oregano, dill seed, mace, lemongrass, tumeric etc. The labels were all written in ye olde worlde-style fonts, stuck on little bottles whose seals remained secure for a decade or two.

This and opposite page, racks in all shapes and sizes – if you had a space in your house, there was a rack to fill it

6

7

8

5

9

10

11

12

13

788

①

depuis

85F

115F

Livré garni.

③

CAFÉ SEL SUCRE

115F

① **49**F90

pour 6 paires

25F

pour 6 paires

Cat flaps

Not to be confused with an intimate area of a woman's body, everyone should have a flap for their pussy fitted into their back door. It's especially useful if you are a cat and cannot reach the door handle, or have not been given a set of door keys. Cat flaps are equally useful as an emergency hatch for sweaty trainers, or as a rubbish shoot for curry leftovers.

The current cat's favourite is the 'Staywell Four Way', which is claimed to be 'suitable for cats of all sizes' and allows you to 'choose the level of freedom you want your cat to have'. For the high-tech moggy, and if stray cats are a problem with cat hooligan gangs getting into your house and raping your timid little darling, then invest in an electro-magnetic locking cat door; your cat wears a small magnetic identity tag which automatically opens the door for your cat. I think they should introduce cat paw-print recognition systems in case some unscrupulous cat robs another's magnetic tag.

You can buy medium and large 'dog doors' for spaniels and poodles, but these could encourage small burglars.

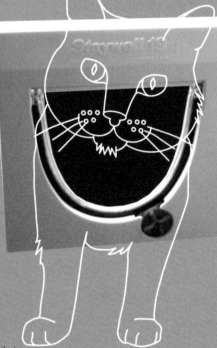

Right, the Staywell cat flap – the moggy's choice

Swing bins

The swing bin is a household icon that students of irony try to reinvent on an annual basis. The reason that their efforts are in vain is that the swing bin is already form-following-function perfection. The lid holds the bin bag securely in position while the lid swings to allow access from two sides. It's wipe-clean, cheap and easy to manufacture. In fact, it's such a sexy design that there are now mini bedside table swing bins for 'intimate' waste.

Above, an integral part of the fitted kitchen; steel or teak-effect bins to match your decor; foot pedals make flip-top bins easy to use; swing bins are just part of a grander storage scheme, including laundry baskets and stools; swing bins are a fine example of form following function

Clotheshorses

Great design is often simple. The Ancient Greeks realised this when the hollow Trojan Horse was devised to hide soldiers during an assault on Troy. Equally inventive in combating another form of warfare – the battle against household drudgery – is the clotheshorse. Perhaps most recognisable grazing in its kitchen habitat, it has been seen in many guises, most commonly as a stout fellow made from timber doweling. Common to all species is one design philosophy: it must give metres of drying rail in a compact space, and be foldable for storage.

Right, *the most common form of clotheshorse is this stout fellow made from wooden doweling*

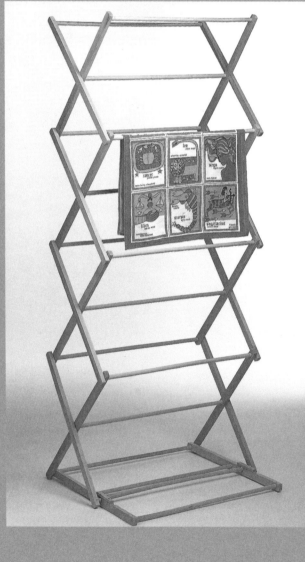

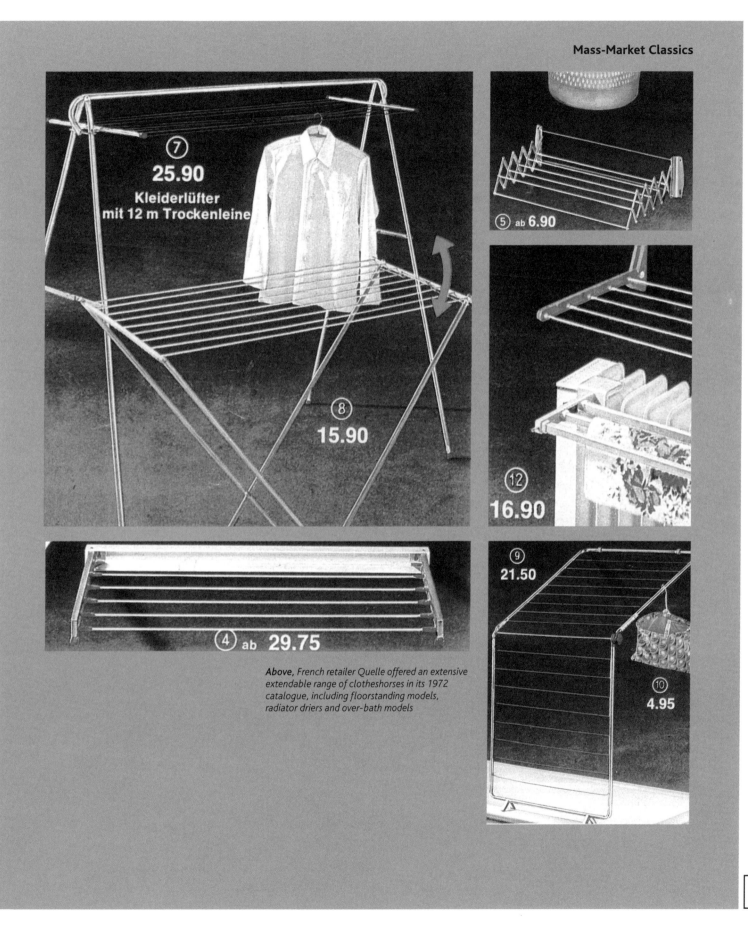

⑦
25.90
Kleiderlüfter
mit 12 m Trockenleine

⑧
15.90

⑤ ab **6.90**

⑫
16.90

④ ab **29.75**

⑨
21.50

⑩
4.95

Above, French retailer Quelle offered an extensive
extendable range of clotheshorses in its 1972
catalogue, including floorstanding models,
radiator driers and over-bath models

Beaded and plastic-strip curtains

Plastic-strip curtains always separated our dining room from the kitchen, and served as a gay and useful screen for the walk-in larder. I say useful because they were supposed to dissuade flies from entering, as these insects apparently have an aversion to multi-coloured, childlike strips of plastic. However, flies in the county of my birth, Lancashire, England, learned to crawl underneath. To help prevent them, we laid multi-coloured striped plastic-covered Kraft yarn rugs on the floor, and this succeeded in putting all but the most audacious beasts off.

Door curtain aficionados would have us believe that their beloved door curtains make a dramatic entrance to a room, while providing privacy without a totally enclosed feeling. But it really is more about flies. Mainland European insects seemed to have an aversion to beaded curtains judging by their choice of doorway decoration. One possible theory is that Europe is close to Africa and thus African beads were used to deter flies.

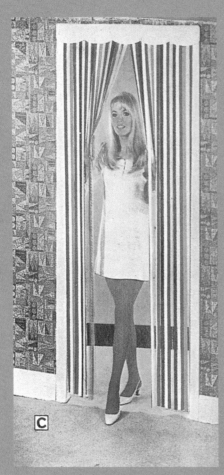

Clockwise from top, what better way to make use of strip curtains than to make a grand entrance dressed in a mini dress? From Freemans catalogue, UK, 1969; beaded curtains were popular in Europe; plastic Kraft yarn rugs were guaranteed to brighten up the dullest of kitchens

Concertina room dividers

In the days before open-plan, it was the done thing to separate our dining and living quarters. The cheapest and most popular method was the concertina divider. With names like the Exclusive Quiet One and Woodgrained Steelite, they glided across our rooms with consummate ease.

LUXURY LIVING AT YOUR FINGERTIPS...

Just a touch and you have one large room for parties or two rooms for comfortable day-to-day living! Superfold is the complete answer to space problems — and you have over 120 patterns and colours to choose from. Write now for fully descriptive leaflet IH 474.

...WITH A **SUPERFOLD** FOLDING PARTITION

The backyard

Our gardens are these days less about producing home-grown vegetables, or providing a bit of grass to lie on. They have become more of a fertile environment for TV makeovers. We see backyards being transformed into scale replicas of Versailles, with water features evoking the Rockies in spring. It's all rot. What they never show are the necessities: rotary driers, loungers and sheds. Here is the pick of the crop...

10

DRYING SPACE: 90 ft
TIDY-SPIN

Rotary airers

This contraption will go down in history as a fine a piece of domestic engineering – both clever and attractive, it must rank as one of the most popular pieces of design ever. No matter how small the space outside your home, there is room for this fold-up baby. The three-arm version gives you 40 metres of line, and the four-armer a whopping great 50 metres, enough to let the wind go to work on four large bath towels, two face cloths, a headscarf, two knitted jerkins, a twinset, three pairs of slacks, a dozen underpants or knickers, ten pairs of socks, six brassieres, a pair of long johns, various tea towels depicting holiday destinations or the British Royal Family, a set of king-size bed sheets and a selection of baby grows.

What is more, this galvanised steel beauty spins in the wind (but you do need to lovingly grease it once a year), its arms can be folded in seconds and it can be lifted and stored in your shed should there be an impending tornado. It can be useful for windsurfers in determining whether it is a 'windsurfing kinda day' and is often used as a selling point in holiday home rentals or property sales.

With names like Tidy Spin, the rotary airer became popular in the mid-1960s when it was sold in the UK's Freemans Home Shopping Catalogue for £6.60 (or 25 pence per week for 34 weeks). Still manufactured in the UK by Beldray, it is just as popular today.

Above, early US versions of this perennial classic, the Tidy Spin and Supa-Dri include sophistication such as 'lift and lock', and some of the larger ones are sized for a US-style wash

Opposite page, the French liked to 'plant a rotary airer' in a field for hippy chic; The Hills version had a sunshade too, making drying clothes a social event

depuis
149,00

TIDY-SPIN SUPA-DRI

EFFORTLESS CLOTHES DRYING AND A SUNSHADE TOO! WITH A *Hills* ROTARY CLOTHES DRIER

79.00
or $5 monthly—

Adult swings

The idea of swaying gently in the breeze in your own backyard has led millions to install garden couches and hammocks. Garden couches, however, are generally uncool, and should only be admired with a healthy dose of irony. If you are brave, then make sure you plump for a garish design, with a fringed canopy and matching sun loungers with fringed roofs, plus a table with fringed cover and umbrella. These should always be accompanied by a skimpily clad blonde.

As usual the Americans took this concept to extremes, developing four-seater 'Glider Settees' that rock and glide, and a four-seater silent swing where couples can face each other. Whatever next?

Those at one with nature, hippies, or simply those who have been on package holidays to Cancun, prefer a string hammock that rots after a rainstorm.

If you can't make up your mind then a floral hammock with a fringe, on two aluminium poles, could just be up your street. Suburbia meets Caribbean beach.

£19·99
53p
for 38 wks

Special offer
SAVE £5·01
Rec'd price £25·00
Our price £19·99

E

③

From top, a double-ended swing chair; every item of garden furniture could be given a fringe; hammocks were for the more adventurous; swings came in bright colours and patterns

Opposite page, what better way to enhance sex appeal than to recline on a floral garden swing?

A

£62·50
£1·65
for 38 wks

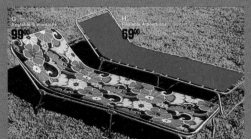

Sun-lounger sets

We're not talking about pool-side loungers made from genuine Californian redwood, but stretch canvas or fold-up loungers upholstered with plastic strips, supported by hollow aluminium legs and a clunky, satisfying four-position ratchet system. If you have never owned one then you are either too rich or an albino with an aversion to sunlight.

The classic design came in plain canvas and in 1977 cost the British 20p per week over 34 weeks or, if you were feeling flush, one payment of £6.75 would net you sunbathing comfort. For the profuse perspirer, replacement covers were available for £1.25. Woven, plastic-strip versions have always been the coolest to look at, but the hottest to sit on.

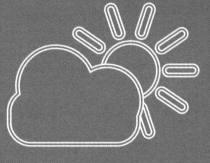

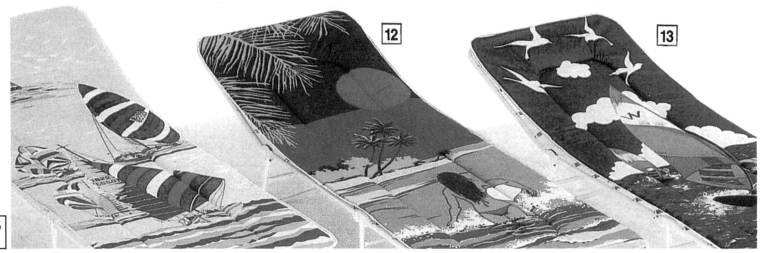

7

8
Tisch
ab **49.**⁹⁰

9
Liegebett
ab **89.**⁵⁰

● Robuste Stahlm
● Platzsparend

5
Gesundheits-
liege,
einzeln
2 Stück
ab **149.–**

Opposite page from top, colourful recliners from French retailer La Redoute, 1976; loungers are adjustable – but mind your fingers; German retailer Schwab offered customers a tropical feel with loungers in 1989

This page from top, ultra-luxurious padded loungers; timber loungers from Sears, 1975

Pirelli rubber strappings

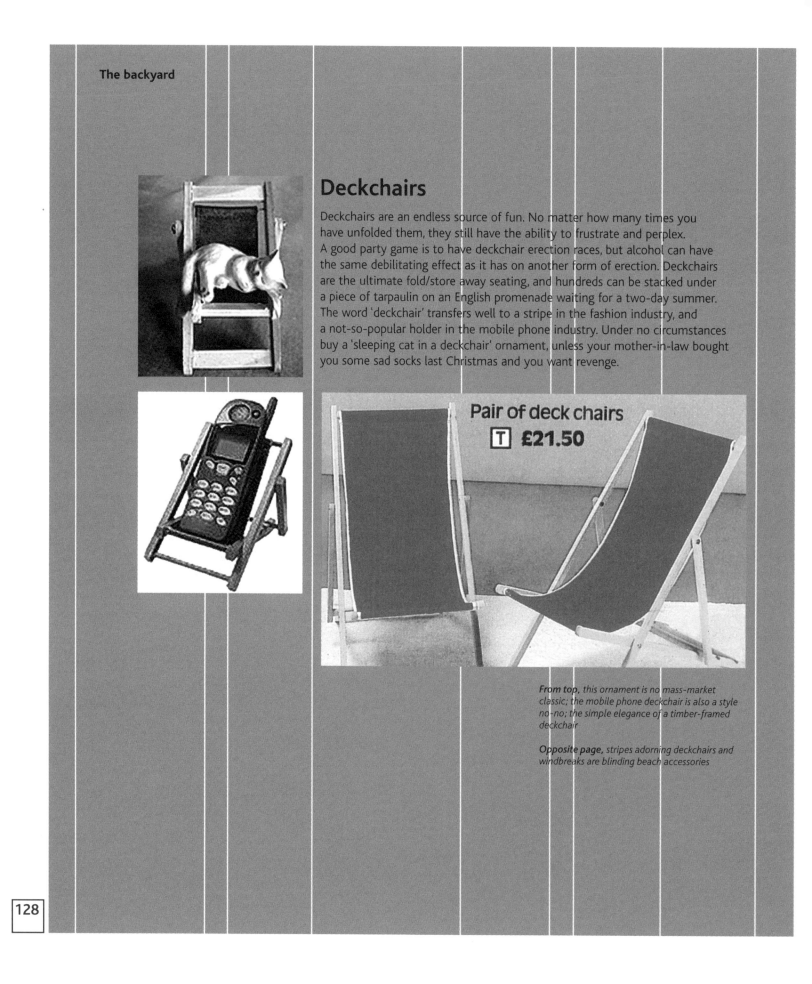

Deckchairs

Deckchairs are an endless source of fun. No matter how many times you have unfolded them, they still have the ability to frustrate and perplex. A good party game is to have deckchair erection races, but alcohol can have the same debilitating effect as it has on another form of erection. Deckchairs are the ultimate fold/store away seating, and hundreds can be stacked under a piece of tarpaulin on an English promenade waiting for a two-day summer. The word 'deckchair' transfers well to a stripe in the fashion industry, and a not-so-popular holder in the mobile phone industry. Under no circumstances buy a 'sleeping cat in a deckchair' ornament, unless your mother-in-law bought you some sad socks last Christmas and you want revenge.

Pair of deck chairs
T £21.50

From top, this ornament is no mass-market classic; the mobile phone deckchair is also a style no-no; the simple elegance of a timber-framed deckchair

Opposite page, stripes adorning deckchairs and windbreaks are blinding beach accessories

B

12 ft DE-LUXE
WINDBREAKER

Special offer

SAVE £1·48
when you buy two
chairs at the same time
for £8·50·
Order MS 551

Woven-plastic garden furniture

Only strange folk get a buzz from sitting with a sweaty backside, or from the pain of flesh welding itself to woven-plastic garden furniture on a hot day. However, woven plastic furniture looks good and the developing world does a jolly sterling job at providing us with this cool-looking garden furniture. From the 1950s capsule-shaped versions with black wrought iron legs, these beauties were affordable when they were introduced and are still affordable today. They are perennials for vintage modernists, like myself, who don't care about designer labels.

The 1960s heralded pre-runners of the nasty modern day white plastic Canal chairs. The difference was that these 1960s' versions are not nasty, they conjure up a nostalgic feeling of pre-Ian Schrager Miami. The curved-arm versions are particularly sought-after.

This decade produced my favourite set of garden furniture ever! Broad strips of different coloured plastic woven onto fold-up loungers. Aesthetically fantastic, affordable and wipe clean, I rest my case. The 1970s saw a rather nastier punched plastic version which was great for leaving temporary tattoos on your back.

Above, *the ultimate in woven-plastic furniture, dating from the 1950s*

Right, *gaily-coloured garden sets from Neckermann, 1964*

Opposite page, *a selection of woven plastic beauties from the 1960s and 1970s*

131

7675
'Chelsea' Wrought Iron   Garden/
Patio Seat. White all weather Vyflex
coated frame. Rec. Retail Price **£24.84**
inc. V.A.T. Write for free brochure to:

G. S. SMART & CO. Ltd., Dept. IH, Moseley Rd.,
Birmingham B12 9BE.   Tel: 021-440 4283

Wrought iron

When I got married in the early 1980s, we bought a white mass-produced five-piece wrought iron garden set. It took pride of place in the back garden for a few years until we self-consciously painted it with blue Hammerite paint to hide its 'pleb' status. But this is not a 'beyond-help' white plastic chair situation.

Wrought iron from the 1950s and 1960s looks very cool, is becoming increasingly collectable and certainly counts as a mass-market classic.

5-pc. umbrella-table set with 4 colorful chair pads
for outdoor dining, party lounging **69⁹⁸** or $5 monthly —see page 164

From top, wrought iron bench by Chelsea, advertised in the UK's Ideal Home magazine, 1975; wrought iron from the 1960s has become very collectable; wrought iron isn't just for furniture – it's ideal for ornamental planters

Opposite page, wrought iron used to add sophistication to a barbeque

Forget trying to get hold of a French 18th century original plant-holder, the mass-produced DIY-store versions are similar in style. The modern ones are also made in rust-free aluminium, but you are still allowed to call it wrought iron – wrought aluminium just doesn't have the same ring.

Go for wrought iron kitsch heaven by accessorising with wrought iron plant-holders, sofas and tree benches.

Above, wrought iron didn't just have outdoor uses, as these products from Sears, 1975, testify

Opposite page, wrought iron could provide a bit of grandeur to any garden

Globe barbecue with even-heat cooking adds the gourmet touch to any meal

Charcoal model

33⁹⁹

- Dome-shaped cover reflects heat for even cooking.
- Dome-shape cooks faster.
- Dome-shape cooks meat on the grill all around—no need for spit.

Save 7.26 patio set and clothes dryer

EATON PRICE

39⁹⁹

cash or 5.00 monthly*

*Use your credit. See p. 338.

Barbecues

Man has been barbecuing for thousands of years – and notice I say 'man' and not 'woman'.

With tongs in one hand and a beer in the other, we dream that we have just killed a woolly mammoth that we are grilling for our family, and that our wives (dressed like Raquel Welch in One Million Years BC) are getting ready to grunt in admiration.

But then it goes wrong: The bottom burns out of the flimsy metal tray holding the briquettes, the flames spread to Raquel's beloved pampas grass and scorch her peonies. She is no longer 'Randy Raquel' as she does what all cavewomen did, and packs you off to the DIY store to buy some bricks.

Left, The styishly pod-like Globe barbecue; the eminently knock-overable standard design

Opposite page, women are only used to sell barbecues – they shouldn't actually use one

Barbecue tips

1. Don't let the wife near you when you are lighting the barbecue. Women don't see the fun of fire and do not get excited by a pile of burning leaves, broken kids' toys, her glossy mags, odd socks and assorted unwanted wedding gifts

2. Buy cheap sausages as they usually contain lots of fat, which catches fire and allows you to play at being a firefighter. If you can lay your hands on a firefighter's uniform then put it on, as this excites the ladies

3. When playing at firefighters, use the contents of your beer bottle. Yes, it is wasteful. No, it doesn't add to the taste but it looks cool

4. Send the little ones around the garden to look for dead spiders, flies, slugs and any dead household pets that they can find. The sizzling of dead insect legs and dead pets' fur is satisfying

Conclusion

I know that I'm biased, but having finished this book and having enjoyed researching and writing it so much, I am more convinced than ever that mass-market products are infinitely cooler, more fun, and have more character than all those overpriced, heavily marketed, so-called designer pieces that fill the pages of myriad glossy magazines and books that clog up retailers' shelves. What's more, you can create a more stimulating and individual home by searching out these pieces, and cherishing and re-using these classics is often a very sustainable and less wasteful option than buying new items.

Acknowledgements

Thanks first and foremost to Keith Stephenson – you are simply the best Graphic Designer, better than all the rest.

Cheers to RotoVision for being a hassle-free publisher – special thanks to Aidan Walker (Boss Man), Luke Herriot (Art Director) and Leonie Taylor (Editor).

Thanks too, to Gareth Gardner for being a great Editor and for looking like Keith.

Respect and gratitude, of course, to all those designers who are unsung heroes for providing us with affordable objects for our homes; and to all those mail order catalogues and retailers (Habitat, Argos, Freemans, Marshall Ward, Graves, Montgomery Ward, Sears, 3 Suisses, etc) that sell us the stuff.

Not forgetting photographer Xavier Young, my researcher Zoe Stanton. Also: Samantha Drinkwater at John Corby Ltd; Carolyn and James at Flying Duck Enterprises, Greenwich; Elliott Prentice at FX magazine; Rebecca Friedrich; and Mark Hampshire.

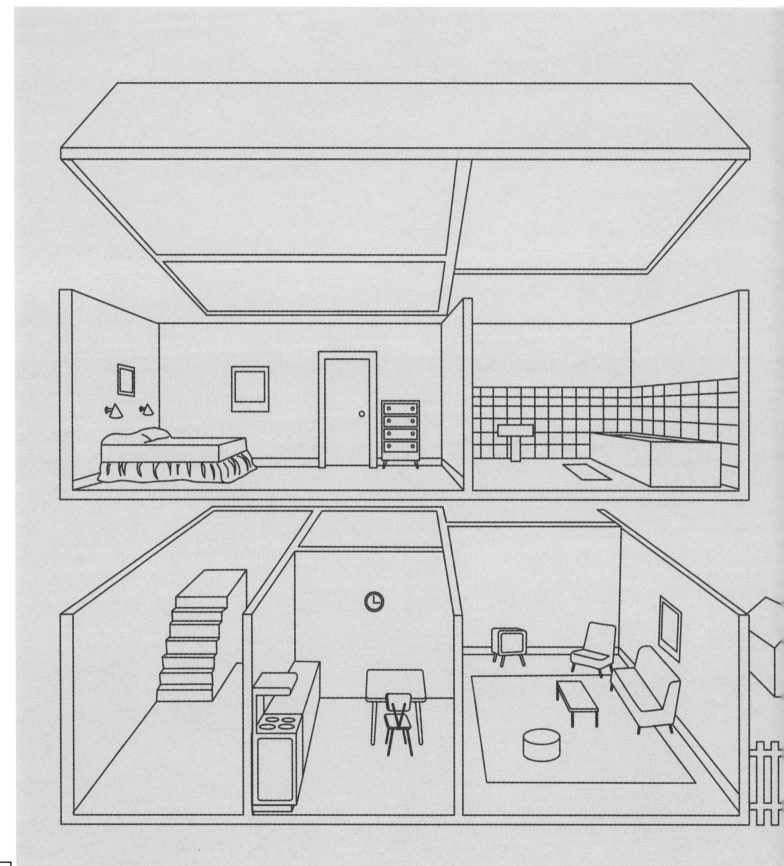

Index

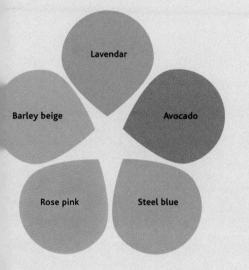

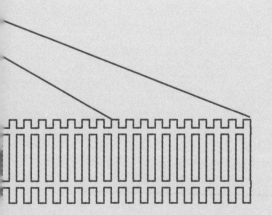